Contemporary Preventive Diplomacy

This book offers an explanation and evaluation of preventive diplomacy in an age of increasing precariousness. It emphasizes the importance of pursuing diplomacy and human security in connection with the Sustainable Development Goals (SDG) which promote development grounded in peace, justice, and universal respect for human rights.

It explores and uncovers efforts to set up diplomatic channels designed to ensure relations between the great powers, intra- and inter-state conflict, terrorism and weapons of mass destruction, human rights, and the global watch over human security do not escalate out of control. Discussing evolving tensions between the United States and China, and the United States and Russia, this book recalls past examples of preventive diplomacy between them, and explores ideas for the exercise of preventive diplomacy in the future. Presenting evidence that contemporary preventive diplomacy is pursued not only by international or regional officials but also by nongovernmental organizations and individuals, the book emphasizes the need to pursue and enhance a comprehensive effort to realize SDG 16 and human security.

The book contains a range of practical recommendations to improve preventive diplomacy and provides a unique optic into understanding the threats facing the planet. It will be of interest to scholars and students of diplomacy, security studies, global governance, and practitioners in government and international organizations.

Bertrand G. Ramcharan of Guyana had a 33-year career at the UN, serving, among other roles, as director in the Department of Political Affairs (Africa I Division), and deputy, then acting High Commissioner for Human Rights. He wrote the first draft of Agenda for Peace, and drafted the recommendation to the secretary-general to establish the UN Preventive Deployment in FYR Macedonia. He has been chancellor of the University of Guyana, professor at the Geneva Graduate Institute of International and Development Studies, member of the Permanent Court of Arbitration, and commissioner of the International Commission of Jurists. He is the author of several books, including *Preventive Diplomacy at the United Nations* and *International Peace Conferences*.

Routledge Global Institutions Series

Edited by Thomas G. Weiss
The CUNY Graduate Center, New York, USA
and Rorden Wilkinson
University of Sussex, Brighton, UK

About the series

The "Global Institutions Series" provides cutting-edge books about many aspects of what we know as "global governance." It emerges from our shared frustrations with the state of available knowledge—electronic and print-wise—for research and teaching. The series is designed as a resource for those interested in exploring issues of international organization and global governance. And since the first volumes appeared in 2005, we have taken significant strides toward filling many conceptual gaps.

The series consists of two related "streams" distinguished by their blue and red covers. The blue volumes, comprising the majority of the books in the series, provide user-friendly and short (usually no more than 50,000 words) but authoritative guides to major global and regional organizations, as well as key issues in the global governance of security, the environment, human rights, poverty, and humanitarian action among others. The books with red covers are designed to present original research and serve as extended and more specialized treatments of issues pertinent for advancing understanding about global governance.

The books in each of the streams are written by experts in the field, ranging from the most senior and respected authors to first-rate scholars at the beginning of their careers. In combination, the components of the series serve as key resources for faculty, students, and practitioners alike. The works in the blue stream have value as core and complementary readings in courses on, among other things, international organization, global governance, international law, international relations, and international political economy; the red volumes allow further reflection and investigation in these and related areas.

The books in the series also provide a segue to the foundation volume that offers the most comprehensive textbook treatment available dealing with all the major issues, approaches, institutions, and actors in contemporary global governance. The second edition of our edited work *International Organization and Global Governance* (2018) contains essays by many of the authors in the series.

Understanding global governance—past, present, and future—is far from a finished journey. The books in this series nonetheless represent significant steps toward a better way of conceiving contemporary problems and issues as well as, hopefully, doing something to improve world order. We value the feedback from our readers and their role in helping shape the on-going development of the series.

A complete list of titles can be viewed online here: www.routledge.com/Global-Institutions/book-series/GI.

Global Business Associations (2019)
Karsten Ronit

A League of Democracies (2019)
Cosmopolitanism, Consolidation Arguments, and Global Public Goods
John Davenport

Moral Obligations and Sovereignty in International Relations (2019)
A Genealogy of Humanitarianism
Andrea Paras

Protecting the Internally Displaced (2019)
Rhetoric and Reality
Phil Orchard

Accessing and Implementing Human Rights and Justice (2019)
Kurt Mills and Melissa Labonte

The IMF, the WTO and the Politics of Economic Surveillance (2019)
Martin Edwards

Multinational Rapid Response Mechanisms (2019)
John Karlsrud and Yf Rykers

Towards a Global Consensus Against Corruption (2019)
International Agreements as Products of Diffusion and Signals of Commitment
Mathis Lohaus

Negotiating Trade in Uncertain Worlds (2019)
Misperception and Contestation in EU-West Africa Relations
Clara Weinhardt

Negotiations in the World Trade Organization (2019)
Design and Performance
Michal Parizek

The International Organization for Migration (2020)
Challenges, Commitments, Complexities
Megan Bradley

Humanitarian Negotiations with Armed Groups (2020)
The Frontlines of Diplomacy
Jonathan Ashley Clements

Diaspora Organizations in International Affairs
Edited by Dennis Dijkzeul and Margit Fauser

Global Think Tanks
Policy Networks and Governance
2nd edition
James G. McGann with Laura C. Whelan

Regionalism under Stress
Europe and Latin America in Comparative Perspective
Edited by Detlef Nolte and Brigitte Weiffen

Contemporary Preventive Diplomacy
Bertrand G. Ramcharan

Contemporary Preventive Diplomacy

Bertrand G. Ramcharan

LONDON AND NEW YORK

First published 2020
by Routledge
2 Park Square, Milton Park, Abingdon, Oxon OX14 4RN

and by Routledge
52 Vanderbilt Avenue, New York, NY 10017

Routledge is an imprint of the Taylor & Francis Group, an informa business

© 2020 Bertrand G. Ramcharan

The right of Bertrand G. Ramcharan to be identified as author of
this work has been asserted by him in accordance with sections 77
and 78 of the Copyright, Designs and Patents Act 1988.

All rights reserved. No part of this book may be reprinted or
reproduced or utilized in any form or by any electronic,
mechanical, or other means, now known or hereafter invented,
including photocopying and recording, or in any information
storage or retrieval system, without permission in writing from the
publishers.

Trademark notice: Product or corporate names may be trademarks
or registered trademarks, and are used only for identification and
explanation without intent to infringe.

British Library Cataloguing-in-Publication Data
A catalogue record for this book is available from the British
Library

Library of Congress Cataloging-in-Publication Data
A catalog record has been requested for this book

ISBN: 978-0-367-25622-7 (hbk)
ISBN: 978-0-429-28872-2 (ebk)

Typeset in Times New Roman
by Wearset Ltd, Boldon, Tyne and Wear

Contents

List of boxes	viii
Foreword	ix
AMBASSADOR TEFERA SHIAWAL	
Preface	xii
Acknowledgments	xv
List of abbreviations	xvii

	Introduction	1
1	The United Nations	8
2	Africa: The AU and sub-regional organizations	42
3	Asia: ASEAN and other sub-regional institutions and proposals	59
4	The Americas and Europe: The OAS and OSCE	75
5	Conclusion: Optimism about civil society, and a proposed executive preventive role for the UN Security Council	95

Select bibliography	109
Index	111

Boxes

1.1	The obligations of governments under the UN Charter	9
1.2	Respect for and protection of human rights as the key to prevention	23
2.1	Cooperation between the African Union and the United Nations	51
3.1	Cooperation between the UN and Asian and European multilateral organizations on combating terrorism	68
4.1	The Tallin Guidelines: Conflict prevention through protection of national minorities and a focus on the role of the media	85
4.2	ODIHR work in relation to democracy, human rights, and the prevention of violence	88
5.1	Preventive engagements in 2018 by the UN Department of Political Affairs (now DPPA)	97
5.2	Greta Thunberg's address at the UN Climate Action Summit, September 23, 2019	99
5.3	Elders support democratic transition in Zimbabwe via a letter to SADC	103

Foreword

Ambassador Tefera Shiawal

Founding Director of the Centre for Dialogue, Research and Cooperation, Addis Ababa

As this book is coming out, the world is undergoing a devastating global pandemic from the coronavirus, with no cure in sight as of the time of writing, with thousands of people killed, hundreds of thousands afflicted, and millions of people locked down inside their homes. This is convincing vindication of one of the principal ideas advanced in this book, namely that the international community must attach urgency to the development of a Comprehensive Global Watch Over Human Security.

In this book, the author presents valuable analyses of contemporary preventive diplomacy in respect of climate change, weapons of mass destruction, conflicts and violence, gross violations of human rights, and the perspectives of Sustainable Development Goal 16, which deals with development, peace, security, justice, the rule of law , respect for human rights, and the entrenchment of strong institutions in all countries. He sees all of these as potentially contributing to the unfolding of a Comprehensive Global Watch Over Human Security.

While there is significant preventive diplomacy taking place at the United Nations and in regional and sub-regional organizations, it is not evident that the perspective of a Comprehensive Global Watch Over Human Security is animating them actively, and it will be important for all of these organizations to sharpen their focus in this respect in the future.

Taking, as an example, the peace and security architecture of the African Union, it is dedicated to the goals of peace, justice, development, and equitable institutions of governance, all of which are highlighted in the UN Sustainable Development Goals, particularly SDG 16, to which Africa subscribes wholeheartedly.

At the Centre for Dialogue, Research and Cooperation based in Addis Ababa, we are ever attentive to situations that might benefit from discreet

x *Foreword*

diplomatic intercession with a view to heading off crisis or conflict, and with a view to advancing the cause of human dignity and rights in Africa. The African Union Commission and Commissioner for Peace and Security, and the members of the AU Panel of the Wise, often extend their good offices in situations of need, and have helped calm difficult situations that might otherwise have spun out of control.

The Conflict Prevention Division of the AU Peace and Security secretariat, and the Situation Room, analyze and bring to the attention of the AU Commissioner for Peace and Security situations where they consider that a discreet AU diplomatic intercession might be useful.

The Chairperson and Members of the AU Peace and Security Council are constantly in diplomatic contacts with leaders in African countries when endeavoring to help calm and defuse situations of concern. From this perspective, the practice of preventive diplomacy is an on-going exercise within the African Union.

Sometimes AU preventive diplomacy is met with success, a phenomenon that, in the nature of things, it usually keeps discreet. On other occasions, preventive diplomacy might be adversely affected by the influence of external powers or by lack of resources.

The AU is ever on the look-out for new ways and means of exercising preventive diplomacy and has recently launched a new initiative that highlights the role of women as ambassadors for peace on the continent. It now has a cadre of female ambassadors for peace, and is adding more and more prominent names to this cadre.

Reinforcing these diplomatic initiatives, the AU has an elaborate normative and institutional architecture that seeks to foster peace in the long term. It has an initiative to silence the guns; norms against weapons of mass destruction; norms on disarmament. And it has development initiatives that seek to anchor peace in sustainable development, justice, and equitable institutions. AU peacekeeping serves the cause of prevention with great dedication.

It would be fair to comment, however, that, lacking UN leadership on taking forward a Comprehensive Global Watch Over Human Security, this orientation is not much in evidence in African Union preventive diplomacy, nor, for that matter, in the other regional organizations discussed in this book, including ASEAN, OAS and OSCE. The UN Secretary-General should urgently convene a meeting of the heads of UN bodies and regional and sub-regional organizations to give impetus to efforts for a Comprehensive Global Watch Over Human Security.

In its discussion of Contemporary Preventive Diplomacy in the world, the present volume considers interesting new initiatives in developmental preventive diplomacy, such as the UN's designation of peace and development

Foreword xi

advisers, and the UN's facilitation of the role of local mediators. This book will certainly stimulate further reflection within international and regional organizations on ways and means of enhancing preventive diplomacy in the future.

The author did extensive field research, including visits to African preventive institutions such as the African Union, ECOWAS, IGAD, and the Centre for Dialogue, Research and Cooperation, in Addis Ababa. It was valuable to exchange views and insights with him during his visit.

The author has previously written *Preventive Diplomacy at the UN* for the UN Intellectual History series and, *Preventive Human Rights Strategies* for Routledge's Global Institutions series. With this volume, he shares further reflections on the future enhancement of preventive diplomacy.

Having served in war and peace, as former Director of the International Conference on the Former Yugoslavia, Director in the UN Department of Political Affairs, UN High Commissioner for Human Rights, Chancellor of the University of Guyana, and Professor at the Geneva Graduate Institute of International and Development Studies, he brings a broad range of experiences to the discussion of contemporary and future preventive diplomacy. For this, we are deeply appreciative.

19 March 2020

Preface

This book is being offered in unprecedented times. Young people are demonstrating by the millions, calling on world leaders to take action to stem global warming. It cannot be taken for granted that national leaders will listen and take corrective action. In the meantime, natural disasters and conflicts directly attributable to climate change are taking a devastating toll on human lives.

Technology has advanced to such a point that humans and computers are already interfacing in many ways, leading to calls for the articulation of new rights to cover this new situation.[1] This is taking place at a time when the global population is exploding, as are poverty, inequality, and discrimination. People are seeking to move across borders by the millions to escape the devastation of global warming, conflicts, violence, and poor governance, and these population flows are causing backlashes and tensions.

Multilateralism is under challenge from powerful national leaders. At the same time, a panel established by the UN secretary-general has called for multilateralism to be complemented by "multi-stakeholderism," embracing not only governments but corporations and IT companies. How all of this will affect the UN in the future remains to be seen.[2]

Jim Al-Khalili, science correspondent at the British Broadcasting Corporation (BBC), has written:

> You can be sure that within a decade or two we will have AI-controlled smart cities, driverless cars, augmented reality, genetically modified food, new and more efficient forms of energy-smart materials, and a myriad of gadgets and appliances all networked and talking to each other. It will be a world almost unrecognizable from today's, just as today's world would appear to someone in the 1970s and 1980s. One thing we can say with certainty is that our lives will continue to be completely transformed by advances in our understanding of how the world works and how we harness it.[3]

Preface xiii

Is it, in these circumstances, still valid to contemplate preventive diplomacy and to study its contemporary and possible future roles? We think it is. The reason is that for the foreseeable future it will still be important to attempt to achieve several key goals: 1. Contain global warming; 2. Control weapons of mass destruction; 3. Head off conflicts and violence; 4. Prevent gross violations of human rights; and 5. Pursue the implementation of Sustainable Development Goal 16 (SDG 16), which is devoted to peace, justice, and strong institutions. These are the five lenses through which we shall look at contemporary preventive diplomacy in this book.

And we shall seek to make the case for the enhancement of a "Global Watch Over Human Security" in the environmental, political, economic, social, developmental, human rights, and humanitarian fields. Some elements of this global watch are already in place, but there is need to bring them together and to reinforce them in the future.

In the Conclusion we shall also make the case for the UN Security Council to exercise more executive responsibilities in a fast-changing world. We are aware that this is a far-reaching proposal, but feel that there is no alternative, and shall explain why.

December 31, 2019

Notes

1 See John Thornhill, "Neural Interfaces Should Upgrade Rather than Degrade Humans," *Financial Times*, September 17, 2019. The author quotes Marcello Ienca, a professor of bioethics at ETH Zurich:

> Mr Ienca supports a new jurisprudence of the mind, establishing a legal framework for this technology. He suggests at least four legal rights need to be enshrined. First, cognitive liberty should protect us from unwanted examination of the mind … Second, mental privacy rights should guarantee that brain data must not be recorded or used without someone's knowledge or shared without consent. Third, mental integrity should be preserved. Neural interface companies, advertisers, armies and governments must not exploit the technology to "brainwash" anyone. Fourth, psychological continuity should ensure that personal identity is not compromised. A company should not disturb, or own, your sense of self.

2 See Anne-Marie Slaughter, "A New Kind of Multilateralism is on the Horizon," *Financial Times*, September 19, 2019. Slaughter writes:

> "Multi-stakeholderism" is not only necessary, but impossible to stop. Digital space does not recognize the elaborate distinctions of power and protocol that governments have spent centuries building and safeguarding …

xiv *Preface*

Digital tools will make global governance with actual global participation possible, even as they create new dangers and challenges. Digital and physical power are already merging in frightening ways. The only way to counter this threat, as in the physical world, is by digital cooperation.

3 Jim Al Khalili, ed., *What's Next?* (London: Profile Books, 2017), 3.

Acknowledgments

I should like to thank Professors Thomas Weiss and Rorden Wilkinson, the editors of this series, for including this book in the Routledge Global Institutions series. I should also like to thank Prof. Weiss's colleagues at the Ralph Bunche Institute for their assistance, and Dr Martin Burke, who helped me improve the presentation.

Robert Sorsby and his colleagues at Routledge greatly facilitated the production of the work and I am grateful to them.

Many members of the UN Department of Political and Peacebuilding Affairs (DPPA) generously provided of their time and insights and I should like to thank them all.

Michele Griffin of the Executive Office of the Secretary-General, and Philippe Baudin-Auliac of the Office of the Director-General in Geneva, both former colleagues of mine, provided encouragement and advice.

I should like to thank Ambassador Smail Chergu, peace and security commissioner of the African Union, and Dr Dawit Toga, political analyst in the AU Conflict Management Division, who both helped me understand the rich preventive diplomacy of the African Union.

Ambassador Hoang Anh Tuan, deputy secretary-general of the Association of Southeast Asian Nations (ASEAN) helped me understand the preventive diplomacy efforts of that organization. ASEAN colleagues Lee Chen Chen and Shafia Muhipat, both leading experts on the ASEAN system of preventive diplomacy, also generously shared their insights with me and provided many useful comments and suggestions for which I am most grateful.

I am also grateful to the members of the Centre for Dialogue, Research and Cooperation, Addis Ababa, who generously gave of their time and insights during my research visit there: Ambassador Tefera Shiawal; Ambassador Abdeta Dribssa Beyene; Ambassador Tekeda Alemu, former permanent representative of Ethiopia to the United Nations and representative on the Security Council; Samrawit Arayamedhin Mersha, communications advisor; and Tirumenich Yimer, executive coordinator.

xvi *Acknowledgments*

Tegiste Hailu, communications officer of the Intergovernmental Authority on Development (IGAD) provided helpful insights and information on the preventive diplomacy of that organization. J.G. Salazar, secretary of the Organization of American States (OAS) Committee on Hemispheric Security, was helpful in providing documents on the work of the committee and in sharing his reflections.

Finally, I should like to thank Dr Robin Ramcharan, director of the Research Institute for Preventive Diplomacy in ASEAN, Bangkok, for his advice and assistance.

Abbreviations

ACCORD	African Centre for the Constructive Resolution of Disputes
ACD	Asian Cooperation Dialogue
AI	Artificial intelligence
AICHR	ASEAN Intergovernmental Commission on Human Rights
ASEAN	Association of Southeast Asian Nations
AU	African Union
AWGCC	ASEAN Working Group on Climate Change
CEWARN	IGAD's Conflict Early Warning and Response Mechanism
DPA	UN Department of Political Affairs
DPPA	UN Department of Political and Peacebuilding Affairs
DRC	Democratic Republic of the Congo
EAS	East Asia Summit
ECCAS	Economic Community of Central African States
ECOSOC	UN Economic and Social Council
ECOWAS	Economic Community of West African States
HCHR	UN high commissioner for human rights
HCNM	OSCE high commissioner on national minorities
IAEA	International Atomic Energy Agency
ICISS	International Commission on Intervention and State Sovereignty
ICRC	International Committee of the Red Cross
IGAD	Intergovernmental Authority on Development
IISS	International Institute of Strategic Studies
IPCC	UN Intergovernmental Panel on Climate Change
ISIS	Islamic State in Iraq and Syria
LRA	Lord's Resistance Army
MDG	Millennium Development Goal
NATO	North Atlantic Treaty Organization
NGO	Nongovernmental organization
OAS	Organization of American States

xviii *Abbreviations*

ODIHR	OSCE Office for Democratic Institutions and Human Rights
OHCHR	Office of the UN High Commissioner for Human Rights
OSCE	Organization for Security and Cooperation in Europe
SADC	Southern African Development Community
SALW	Small arms and light weapons
SCO	Shanghai Cooperation Organization
SDG	Sustainable Development Goal
SIPRI	Stockholm International Peace Research Institute
SSR	Security sector reform
UDHR	Universal Declaration of Human Rights
UN	United Nations
UNDP	UN Development Programme
UNHCHR	UN High Commissioner for Human Rights
UNHCR	UN High Commissioner for Refugees
UNHRC	UN Human Rights Council
UNOCA	UN Office for Central Africa
UNODA	UN Office for Disarmament Affairs
UNOWAS	UN Office for West Africa and the Sahel
UNRCCA	UN Regional Centre for Preventive Diplomacy in Central Asia
WMD	Weapon of mass destruction

Introduction

A quarter of a century after the issuance of United Nations Secretary-General Boutros Boutros-Ghali's *An Agenda for Peace*,[1] the concept of preventive diplomacy has evolved dramatically, and a modern concept is now in evidence in international relations. It is, in simple terms, diplomacy with a preventive purpose or orientation, and it is applied not only to disputes or conflicts but to a broad range of issues and problems affecting the survival and welfare of humankind. The constituent elements are literally prevention and diplomacy. It may be public diplomacy or discreet diplomacy. And, what has emerged forcefully from the actions of young people to help save the planet from global warming, it may be preventive diplomacy deployed by individuals or groups.

Preventive diplomacy now extends beyond disputes and conflicts to the sensitization of the international community to threats and challenges to the survival and security of humanity; to the articulation and pursuit of policies to deal with those threats; and to the emplacement of laws and institutions to deal with global problems affecting the welfare of humanity, such as gross human rights violations, climate change, weapons of mass destruction, disarmament, sustainable development, and human security broadly. Preventive diplomacy is exercised by global and national leaders, international officials, leaders of nongovernmental organizations (NGOs), and a wide range of other actors.

Preventive diplomacy is a process. Even if success is elusive in the short term, it can still help mitigate situations or it can offer a vision of the future that rallies consensus eventually. Preventive diplomacy and conflict management are sometimes two sides of the same coin.

To compare the contemporary concept with that of 1992, we may recall that *An Agenda for Peace* defined preventive diplomacy as "action to prevent disputes from arising between parties, to prevent existing disputes from escalating into conflicts and to limit the spread of the latter when they occur." The aims of United Nations action, it added, were "[t]o seek to identify at the earliest possible stage situations that could produce conflict and

2 *Introduction*

to try through diplomacy to remove the sources of danger before violence results." The spheres of action were disputes and conflicts. Contemporary preventive diplomacy goes well beyond these.

Global developments have necessitated the development of new forms of preventive diplomacy as the challenges of prevention, and of preventive diplomacy, become more complex. For example, global warming has made some wars more likely, and will make others more so in the future: seasonal rains and monsoons are becoming more variable and less predictable, and as one area grows parched, its inhabitants encroach on land traditionally farmed or used for grazing by others. Disputes in turn erupt, some of which are already turning violent. Climate-induced war is a major reason for governments to take global warming seriously.[2]

Such concerns are gaining traction. In May 2018, UN Secretary-General Antonio Guterres, for example, in launching his disarmament agenda, titled "Securing Our Common Future: An Agenda for Disarmament," cautioned:

> [w]e are living in dangerous times. Cold War tensions are back, global military spending is at its highest and protracted conflicts are causing unspeakable human suffering. This is why I launched my disarmament agenda ... Disarmament prevents and ends violence. Disarmament supports sustainable development. And disarmament is true to our values and principles.[3]

A recent book by Bill McKibben, *Falter*, asks the question, "Has the human game begun to play itself out?" McKibben surveyed the state of the world and found that even as climate change shrinks the space where human civilization can exist, new technologies like artificial intelligence, robotics, and life-prolonging treatments threaten to "bleach away the variety of human experience." The author warns of the risks of nuclear war and multiple hazards associated with climate change, increasing atmospheric carbon dioxide, threats to food production, rising sea levels, and ocean warming and acidification.[4] There are also forces opposing solutions to these problems, motivated by self-interest, grim realities, power, ideas, and views about the proper role of government.[5]

In the face of the dire threats facing humanity, a study of contemporary preventive diplomacy needs to consider five central sets of issues: climate change, weapons of mass destruction, conflicts and violence, gross violations of human rights, and the promise of Sustainable Development Goal 16, the latter of which is dedicated to the promotion of sustainable development, peace, justice, and strong, equitable institutions.[6]

Climate change represents perhaps the most serious threat to human security. The United Nations has sought to alert the world to the dangers

Introduction 3

involved, to promote international agreements, and to encourage their implementation. But not all governments see eye to eye on the risks, and the UN secretary-general is deploying his best endeavors on the issue, including through the designation of a special envoy on the subject to engage in diplomatic efforts on behalf of stronger international cooperation. Secretary-General Guterres is undoubtedly an active and passionate champion of preventive diplomacy.

Weapons of mass destruction also pose acute dangers, be they nuclear, biological, or chemical. Ever since its establishment, the UN has sought to promote disarmament, and there is a measure of public diplomacy in the deliberations of the Security Council, the General Assembly, and the Conference on Disarmament. Secretary-General Guterres' new disarmament agenda, mentioned above, seeks to revitalize this process.[7] Aspirational preventive diplomacy may be seen at work here.

Conflicts and violence, on an unprecedented scale, continue to be felt in many parts of the world and often do engage the attention of the United Nations as well as regional and sub-regional organizations. In similar vein, gross violations of human rights result in widespread loss of life and human suffering, but the UN and regional organizations have rarely been able to prevent or stop such violations, or even to stem the tide of gross violations.

The report of the International Commission on Intervention and State Sovereignty (ICISS) launched the concept of "the responsibility to protect" in 2001.[8] In the commission's view, the responsibility to protect embraces three specific responsibilities. First, the responsibility to prevent, namely, to address both the root causes and direct causes of internal conflict and other man-made crises putting populations at risk. Second, the responsibility to react, that is to respond to situations of compelling human need with appropriate measures, which may include coercive actions such as sanctions and international prosecution, and in extreme cases military intervention. And third, the responsibility to rebuild, namely, to provide, particularly after a military intervention, full assistance with recovery, reconstruction, and reconciliation, addressing the causes of the harm the intervention was designed to halt or avert.

The commission was firm in its view that prevention is the single most important dimension of the responsibility to protect. Prevention options should always be exhausted before intervention is contemplated, and more commitment and resources must be devoted to it. The exercise of the responsibility to prevent and react should always involve less intrusive and coercive measures before others are applied.

While there is some diplomacy to prevent gross violations of human rights, such as the efforts of the Organization for Security and Cooperation in Europe's (OSCE's) office of the High Commissioner on National

4 *Introduction*

Minorities (HCNM), and the secretary-general's special adviser on the prevention of genocide, there is need for considerably more. The main problem is not one of lack of information, or know-how, but of political obstacles. Governments and nonstate actors that violate human rights are rarely receptive to diplomacy to prevent the violations. The challenge is to try out approaches that might possibly help bring about the receptivity of these actors to intercessions that could help head off violations.

Of the seven sets of international, regional, and sub-regional organizations discussed in this book, the OSCE has institutions explicitly devoted to the protection of minorities and the prevention of gross violations of human rights. The office of the HCNM has, for more than a quarter of a century, pioneered efforts to defuse conflicts grounded in ethnic tensions or minority grievances. We discuss the HCNM later in the book. Furthermore, the OSCE Office for Democratic Institutions and Human Rights (ODIHR) has a pronounced preventive rationale through its work in observing elections to assess compliance with the OSCE's election standards; and promoting strengthening of the rule of law through assistance in achieving compliance with the organization's commitments regarding judicial independence, access to the legal profession and justice, and criminal justice in general.[9]

The African Union, the Association of Southeast Asian Nations (ASEAN), and the Organization of American States (OAS) would be well advised to consider establishing institutions similar to the office of the OSCE high commissioner and ODIHR.

Faced with the scale of conflicts, violence, and gross violations of human rights worldwide, the UN 2030 Agenda for Sustainable Development and the 17 Sustainable Development Goals (SDGs), particularly SDG 16, have highlighted the importance of working for peace, justice, inclusive societies, and strong institutions. The preventive aspirations of SDG 16 are widely recognized, and the UN community, including civil society, is developing and applying indicators of varying types to measure its implementation. One NGO, the Fund for Peace, publishes an annual report on countries at risk of conflict. This is important work, but it remains to be seen how it will contribute tangibly to UN action for the prevention of conflicts and violence.

In this book we shall seek to study to what extent, and how, the UN, the African Union and sub-regional African institutions, ASEAN and some institutions in the Middle East and wider Asia region, and the OAS and OSCE engage in contemporary preventive diplomacy in relation to our five priority themes: climate change, weapons of mass destruction, conflicts and violence, gross violations of human rights, and SDG 16. The organizations discussed all have a long history of programs and processes to engage in preventive diplomacy efforts.

Introduction 5

The UN has a long history of efforts for preventive diplomacy.[10] The African Union also has a peace and security architecture, with a Peace and Security Council at its apex. The AU constitution provides explicitly for African Union intervention in situations of crisis to help head off or mitigate human suffering and to help resolve crises. Several African subregional organizations—the Economic Community of West African States (ECOWAS), the Intergovernmental Authority on Development (IGAD), and the Southern African Development Community (SADC)—have elaborate blueprints for conflict prevention.

In Asia, ASEAN's annual Regional Forum has, for years, brought together member states and other leading powers for discussions on cooperation for conflict avoidance. The ASEAN Constitution provides significant competence for its secretary-general and competent bodies to act urgently to head off or mitigate potential crises. The Arab League, the oldest of the sub-regional organizations in Asia, has less of a practice in this matter and we discuss it briefly in the Asia chapter. As far as that continent is concerned, we have in mind particularly the recurring dangers of conflict in the Persian Gulf and the tense stand-off between two nucleararmed powers, India and Pakistan.

In terms of the Americas and Europe, the OAS, since its establishment, has had machinery for prevention and peacemaking, and has a particularly interesting organ, the Committee on Hemispheric Security. Conflict prevention has also been one of the high priorities of the OSCE since its establishment.

In discussing our five selected themes, we shall have in mind normative and policy frameworks where they exist, the practice of the institutions concerned, and desirable policy innovations where this might be useful. This is particularly the case when it comes to efforts to head off gross violations of human rights. There is a paucity of preventive approaches for dealing with human rights issues in most of the institutions discussed in this book. While identifying such preventive strands as may exist, the book will argue that there is need to develop a policy framework in this area and we shall make suggestions in this regard.

The human rights regimes of the UN, the AU, ASEAN, the OAS, and the OSCE turn around reporting systems, petitions, and fact-finding procedures, and two prevention institutions in the latter case, as mentioned above. In the future it will be necessary to rethink the core strategies of the human rights regimes of the AU, ASEAN, and the OAS so as to provide them with a more explicit preventive orientation.

At the UN, the Office of High Commissioner for Human Rights (OHCHR) should take on the role of the human rights component of a global watch over human security. In Africa, a more proactive approach is

6 *Introduction*

required for the protection of minorities, and the AU should consider the appointment of an office of high commissioner on national minorities similar to that of the OSCE. In Asia and Latin America, more proactive approaches are required for the protection of indigenous peoples. New thinking is required here. In Europe, there will be a need to think how the OSCE Office for Democratic Institutions and Human Rights can play a role in spearheading programs for the protection of ethnic groups. These regional regimes could learn from the methods and approaches of the International Crisis Group.

Chapter 1 of this book discusses the work of the United Nations. The following three chapters examine one or more regions of the world, focusing on the preventive work of some major regional and sub-regional organizations. Chapter 2 looks at the primary African organizations, the AU, ECOWAS, IGAD, and SADC. Chapter 3 focuses on Asia, primarily analyzing the role of ASEAN, but also that of the Arab League and a few minor initiatives. Chapter 4, on the Americas and Europe, examines the work of the OAS and OSCE.

Finally, Chapter 5 summarizes the book's findings on the role of intergovernmental organizations, and discusses preventive diplomacy activities by civil society groups and individuals. It then offers some concluding observations and a proposal involving the UN Security Council. It will be our submission that the threats to the future of humanity are such that a core part of future preventive strategies must be to develop a new international law of security and protection anchored in an executive role for the council. While this is a far-reaching idea, security and protection must define the international cooperation and law of the future.

Notes

1 Boutros Boutros-Ghali, *An Agenda for Peace* (New York: United Nations, 1992). This author wrote the first draft of the report.
2 *The Economist*, "How to Think about Global Warming and War: They Are Linked—and That Is Worrying," May 23, 2019, 15–16, www.economist.com/leaders/2019/05/23/how-to-think-about-global-warming-and-war.
3 UN News, "UN Chief Launches New Disarmament Agenda 'to Secure Our World and Our Future,'" May 24, 2018, https://news.un.org.
4 Bill McKibben, *Falter: Has the Human Game Begun to Play itself Out?* (New York: Henry Holt, 2019), 11.
5 See Jared Diamond, "How It Ends," *New York Times* book review, April 21, 2019.
6 See on this Jeffrey D. Sachs, *The Age of Sustainable Development* (New York: Columbia University Press, 2015).
7 See Rachel Bronson, "A New Age of Nuclear Instability," *New York Times International Edition*, February 5, 2019.

Introduction 7

8 ICISS, *The Responsibility to Protect* (Ottawa: International Development Research Centre, 2001). See also Thomas G. Weiss and Don Hubert, *The Responsibility to Protect: Research, Bibliography, Background*, Supplementary Volume to the Report of the International Commission on Intervention and State Sovereignty (Ottawa: ICISS, 2001).

9 See OSCE Office for Democratic Institutions and Human Rights, OSCE.org/odihr.

10 See on this Bertrand Ramcharan, *Preventive Diplomacy at the UN* (Bloomington: Indiana University Press, 2008).

1 The United Nations

- Climate change
- Weapons of mass destruction
- Conflicts and violence
- Human rights
- SDG 16
- Conclusion

United Nations preventive diplomacy is inspiring in some instances, dynamic in areas such as climate change, original in providing peace and development advisers, persistent in the endeavors of its sub-regional centers for preventive diplomacy, inventive in the activities of its political department, frustrating in the recalcitrance of many governments (including great powers on the Security Council), and searing in its inability to prevent gross violations of human rights. Yet the purposes of the United Nations, as set out in the UN Charter and the General Assembly's 1970 "Declaration on Principles of International Law concerning Friendly Relations and Cooperation among States," are exactly to coordinate action to achieve common goals in these and other areas. See Box 1.1 below for details on the declaration.

Sustainable Development Goal 16 was meant to encourage a philosophy of development grounded in peace, justice, human rights, and inclusive, equitable, and strong societies, but it has so far not made its mark. In the midst of all of this, the UN secretary-general deploys his best endeavors, to the extent that political circumstances allow. Civil society is mobilizing to help protect the planet, and this is a new form of people-based preventive diplomacy.

The UN's Intergovernmental Panel on Climate Change (IPCC) and the UN secretary-general are the foremost practitioners of preventive diplomacy in the world today, dealing, as they do, with the gravest threat to humanity, providing international alerts and policy recommendations for

The United Nations 9

Box 1.1 The obligations of governments under the UN Charter

According to the very first article of the United Nations Charter, the purposes of the United Nations are, among others, to achieve international cooperation in solving international problems of an economic, social, cultural, or humanitarian character and in promoting and encouraging respect for human rights, and for fundamental freedoms for all without distinction as to race, language, sex, or religion and to be a center for harmonizing the action of nations in the attainment of these common ends. Article 55 of the UN Charter gives the organization a mandate to promote universal respect for and observance of human rights and fundamental freedoms for all. In Article 56, all members pledge themselves to take joint and separate action in cooperation with the UN for the achievement of the purposes set forth in the previous article.

In Resolution 26/25 (XXV) of October 24, 1970, the UN General Assembly adopted "the Declaration on Principles of International Law concerning Friendly Relations and Cooperation among States in accordance with the Charter of the United Nations."[1] This is considered a codification of the legal principles of the charter. In the declaration the General Assembly proclaimed that states have the duty to cooperate with one another, irrespective of the differences in their political, economic and social systems, in the various spheres of international relations in order to maintain international peace and security and to promote international stability and progress, the general welfare of nations, and international cooperation free from discrimination based on such differences.

Source: The author

Note
1 For the text of the declaration, see: https://legal.un.org/avl/pdf/ha/dpilfrcscun/dpilfrcscun_ph_e.pdf.

---

action, and engaging more broadly in global advocacy for preventive and corrective actions. The work of the IPCC provides stunning evidence in support of the concept of contemporary preventive diplomacy presented in the Introduction to this book.

This contemporary concept is much in evidence as the UN seeks to turn around the risks from climate change and weapons of mass destruction, to stem the tide of conflicts and violence, and to reduce gross violations of human rights. We discuss each of these areas in this chapter. As we will see, despite the best efforts of the UN secretary-general and the secretariat, the world organization continues to be constrained by its own governments—some powerful, some recalcitrant, many undemocratic, and many oppressive.

10   *The United Nations*

Climate change

In 2019, the IPCC published a *Special Report on Climate Change and Land*, authored by 107 experts from 52 countries. The report warned that the world's land and water resources are being exploited at unprecedented rates, which, combined with climate change, is putting dire pressure on the ability of humanity to feed itself. This warning comes a year after the IPCC's alarm-raising 1.5 degrees centigrade report, which found that the world needs to take urgent transformative action to avert the worst impacts of climate change beyond 1.5 degrees centigrade warming.[1]

As the 2019 report notes, the window to address the threat from overuse of land and water resources is closing rapidly. A half-billion people already live in places that are turning into deserts, and soil is being lost at between 10 and 100 times faster than it is forming. A particular danger is that food crises may develop on several continents at once, according to Cynthia Rosenzweig, one of the report's authors: "The potential risk of multi-breadbasket failure is increasing. All of these things are happening at the same time."[2] If this is not preventive diplomacy, then what else is?

In September 2019, during the week of the UN Climate Action Summit, the IPCC released a report stating that sea-level rise is accelerating faster than scientists had predicted, putting hundreds of millions of people at risk.[3] According to Nathan Bindoff of the University of Tasmania, one of the report's authors: "Since 1993 the rate of warming of the global oceans has actually doubled—and the rate of warming is a contributor to the acceleration that we see in sea level rise." As reported by another author, Hamish Pritchard of the British Antarctic Survey: "Megacities and low-lying Pacific islands are under threat. This will displace a lot of people." With about 680 million people around the world living in low-lying areas, they could all be threatened by cyclonic winds, coastal erosion, flooding, and waves.[4]

As mentioned in the Introduction, global warming has made some wars more likely than they would otherwise have been and will make others more so in the future. Some experts already worry that the Arctic could be a flashpoint. As the icecaps shrink, the North Atlantic Treaty Organization (NATO) and Russia are currently bolstering their military presence there and China is building a nuclear-powered ice-breaker. Accidents can happen.

Accumulating greenhouse gases in the atmosphere are increasing the frequency and intensity of extreme droughts and floods in some regions. Seasonal rains and monsoons are becoming more variable and less predictable. As one area grows parched, its inhabitants encroach on land traditionally farmed or used for grazing by others, leading to disputes, some of

The United Nations   11

which are turning violent, especially in the Sahel. Environmental stress has already played a role in deadly conflicts in Burkina Faso, Chad, Cameroon, Mali, Niger, northern Nigeria, and South Sudan, as well as in states outside Africa such as Yemen.

Climate-induced war is a reason for governments to take global warming seriously. Since climate change will make some areas uninhabitable, many will migrate to towns or cities in their own country. Moving is a rational way to adapt to a changing environment. Governments should manage the influx, including by building roads and schools to accommodate the newcomers. Unless carefully managed, conflicts will ensue.[5]

In September 2019, UN Secretary-General Antonio Guterres convened a climate summit to bring world leaders, the private sector, and civil society together to support the multilateral process and to increase and accelerate climate action and ambition. The summit focused on key sectors where action could make the most difference—heavy industry, nature-based solutions, cities, energy resilience, and climate finance. World leaders reported on what they were doing and what more they intended to do by the time of the 2020 UN Climate Change Conference, where commitments are expected to be renewed and possibly increased.

Guterres had decided to call on world leaders to come to New York in view of the gravity of the situation of accelerating global emissions, with concrete, realistic plans to enhance their nationally-determined contributions by 2020, in line with reducing greenhouse gas emissions by 45 percent over the next decade, and to net zero emissions by 2050. Guterres acted because global emissions are reaching record levels and show no signs of peaking. The previous four years were the hottest on record, and winter temperatures in the Arctic had risen by 3°C since 1990. Sea levels are rising, coral reefs are dying, and the world is starting to see the life-threatening impact of climate change on health, through air pollution, heatwaves, and risks to food security. The impacts of climate change are being felt everywhere and are having very real consequences on people's lives.[6]

The secretary-general's special envoy for the 2019 Climate Action Summit, former Mexican diplomat Luis Alfonso de Alba, worked energetically to help ensure that the world had the tools, the vision, and the political will necessary to move forward on ambitious climate action for the benefit of all aspects of society. De Alba considered his task as being outreach to governments and the private sector, the raising of awareness, and "rais[ing] the level of the political discussion." The world needs, he argues, "to have a common understanding on the benefits of acting quickly and in a coordinated manner. We need to develop a sense of collective responsibility because this is a problem that cannot be solved by one country alone."[7]

12 *The United Nations*

Consequently, the summit brought together governments, the private sector, civil society, local authorities, and international organizations to develop ambitious solutions in six areas: a global transition to renewable energy, sustainable and resilient infrastructures and cities, sustainable agriculture, management of forests and oceans, resilience and adaptation to climate impacts, and alignment of public and private finances with a net "zero economy."

The summit focused on nine interdependent tracks: (1) Enhancing climate mitigation of major emitting countries; (2) Social and political drivers, such as health, gender, and security; (3) Youth and public mobilization, streamlining youth participation across all related topics; (4) Energy transition, including boosting renewables, energy efficiency, and storage; (5) Industry transition, creating stronger commitment from emissions-heavy sectors such as steel and cement; (6) Infrastructure, cities and local action, to scale up ambitious commitments on low-emission and climate-resilient infrastructure; (7) Nature-based solutions, focusing on areas such as forests, smart agriculture, and oceans; (8) Resilience and adaptation, focusing on integrating climate risks into public and private decision-making; and (9) Climate finance and carbon-pricing, directing finance toward climate-resilient development.[8]

The summit saw the launch of several initiatives designed to boost nature-based solutions. These include a Global Campaign for Nature, which plans to conserve around 30 percent of the Earth's lands and oceans by 2030; a High-Level Panel for the Sustainable Ocean Economy, which will work to build resilience for the ocean and marine-protected areas; a Central African Forest Initiative that aims to protect the region's forest cover (which provides livelihoods for some 60 million people); and a Zero Carbon Building for All initiative aimed at making all buildings—new and existing—net zero carbon by 2050.

Also, as a result of the summit, some 2,000 cities have committed to placing climate risk at the center of their decision-making, planning, and investments. For example, tackling traffic congestion and pollution is the aim of the Action Towards Climate-Friendly Transport Initiative, which includes actions to plan city development in a way that minimizes travel, generates a shift from fossil-fueled vehicles to non-motorized and public transport, and increases the use of zero-emission technologies.[9]

It would be instructive at this point to take note of what the role has been of the Security Council, in theory the premier security organ of the UN. This is relevant to the submission we shall make in the concluding chapter that the world is now at a point when executive action will be needed to protect the earth and its inhabitants. The Security Council is the only organ in the UN with the authority to undertake such executive

The United Nations 13

action. In recent years, the council has held debates on the topic of climate change, seeking to highlight the security risks from global warming and to generate international cooperation to contain and hopefully reverse them. Among other innovations has been the establishment, at the initiative of Germany, of a group of countries concerting their efforts on this problem.

The Security Council discussed climate change for the first time in April 2007. On that occasion views had been divided on whether this was a proper topic for the council. It next discussed the issue in July 2011. Again, views were divided. Related meetings were held in November 2011, July 2015, and November 2016. Some informal, "Arria-formula" meetings were also held in the intervening period.[10]

At the most recent Security Council meeting on the topic, in January 2019, over 70 member states participated, and statements were made in the debate by a dozen ministers. Addressing the meeting, the UN under-secretary-general for political, peacebuilding, and electoral affairs called for attention to be given to key issues such as the development of stronger analytical capacity with integrated risk assessment frameworks; collecting and developing a stronger evidence base so that good practices on climate risk prevention and management could be replicated in the field; and building and reinforcing partnerships to leverage existing capacities within and outside the UN system.

A youth representative and researcher on environmental security, Lindsay Getschel, spoke in the debate, calling on the Security Council to adopt a resolution officially recognizing climate change as a threat to international peace and security. She also called on the council to commission an assessment on how climate change impacts local youth, through, for example, displacement, unemployment, food insecurity, and recruitment in armed groups. She urged the council to agree on a reduction of reliance on fossil fuel energy in UN missions worldwide and a commitment that 50 percent of energy used would be from renewable sources by 2025, with regular reporting to the secretary-general to monitor progress. It would be fair to comment that, faced with the security risks from climate change, the Security Council has so far not been willing to take on an executive role for the protection of humanity, something that, in our submission, it will be required to do in the very near future.

Weapons of mass destruction

In launching his agenda for disarmament, Securing Our Common Future, in May 2018, Secretary-General Guterres cautioned that the world was living in dangerous times. Cold War tensions are back, global military spending is at its highest and protracted conflicts are causing unspeakable

14 *The United Nations*

human suffering. That was why he had decided to launch his agenda: "Disarmament prevents and ends violence. Disarmament supports sustainable development. And disarmament is true to our values and principles."[11] Consequently, his agenda aims at reviving serious multilateral dialogue and bringing disarmament and non-proliferation back to the center of the work of the United Nations.[12]

The disarmament agenda outlines practical measures across the range of disarmament issues, including weapons of mass destruction, conventional arms, and new weapon technologies. It seeks to generate fresh perspectives, create new momentum, and explore areas where serious dialogue is required to bring disarmament back to the heart of common efforts for peace and security. To accomplish these goals, the agenda integrates disarmament into the priorities of the entire United Nations system, laying the foundations for new partnerships and greater collaboration among different parts of the organization and governments, civil society, the private sector, and others.

Securing Our Common Future rests on four pillars. First, "disarmament to save humanity": the existence of nuclear weapons poses a continuing threat to the world, and their total elimination can only be achieved through reinvigorated dialogue and serious negotiations. Second, "disarmament that saves lives": as armed conflicts grow more deadly, destructive, and complex, the world needs a new focus on mitigating the humanitarian impact of conventional arms and providing for more effective regulation. International approaches to arms regulation need to be brought in line with the magnitude of these problems and integrated into broader work for prevention and sustainable development.

Third, "disarmament for future generations": as advances in science and technology continue to revolutionize human life, the world must remain vigilant in its understanding of new and emerging weapons technologies. Fourth, "strengthening partnerships for disarmament": the existing multilateral disarmament institutions need to be reinvigorated and better utilized, through increased use of political will and by improving coordination and integration of expertise into their work. The United Nations and regional organizations should work together to strengthen existing platforms for regional dialogue on security and arms control.

On the crucial issue of implementation, the UN Office for Disarmament Affairs (UNODA) states that its disarmament agenda plan details the activities that UN entities will undertake in order to carry out the 40 actions the agenda contains:

> The implementation plan will be a living document. As work progresses, new steps and activities will be added as needed. The status

The United Nations   15

of activities will be updated on a regular basis, and links to specific outputs will be uploaded on the page for each action.[13]

Securing Our Common Future brings back to mind former Secretary-General Boutros Boutros-Ghali's Agenda for Peace; his Agenda for Development; and his Agenda for Democracy. While the report *An Agenda for Peace* has had lasting significance in the philosophy and doctrines of the UN about preventive diplomacy, the other two have left little imprint on world affairs. It remains to be seen whether Guterres's agenda will gain traction in light of the attitudes of major powers. It is legitimate to ask: can action by entities within the UN system move the powerful governments concerned to cooperate in the implementation of Securing Our Common Future? Will idealism move realism? The agenda lives in hope.

Conflicts and violence

In his 2018 Annual Report, Secretary-General Guterres recalled that he had:

> articulated the idea of a prevention platform with the aim not of creating new structures or processes, but rather as an informal organizational tool designed to enable us to make maximum use of existing resources and capacities in support of a broader prevention agenda that is commensurate with the risks and challenges our Member States are facing.

Preventive diplomacy was front and center in a Security Council debate in November 2018 on "Strengthening Multilateralism and the Role of the United Nations." Guterres encouraged the Security Council to "embrace the prevention and peacebuilding agendas, and make greater use of mediation and the other tools set out in Chapter VI of the UN Charter for the resolution of dispute through peaceful means." The secretary-general was in exhortatory mode.

Many speakers at the council debate highlighted the issue of prevention, calling on the secretary-general to make use of his authority under Article 99 to draw situations of concern to the council's attention, and urging it to draw upon its competence under Chapter VI to investigate and act earlier in situations of concern. They also attached importance to cooperation with regional and sub-regional organizations. The interdependence of peace, development, and human rights was also mentioned by a number of representatives.

What, concretely, might be envisaged to enhance UN preventive diplomacy? To answer this, we should note the ten preventive strategies currently in

16 *The United Nations*

use.[14] First, the secretary-general may intercede discreetly behind the scenes when he considers it advisable to help defuse situations. Second, he may invoke Article 99, but has not yet done so during his tenure (his predecessors did not do this often). Third, he may raise concerns about a situation during his monthly luncheon with members of the Security Council. Fourth, the secretariat may draw the attention of the Security Council to situations of concern in informal consultations. Fifth, there has existed for some time a Mediation Unit in the secretariat whose task is to promote and service the role of mediators to help prevent or defuse crises.

Sixth, there are three sub-regional field offices promoting preventive actions and covering West Africa and the Sahel, Central Africa, and Central Asia. The contributions of these offices have been highly valued, centering on discreet facilitatory actions on the ground. Suggestions have been around for a while to have additional regional offices focusing on prevention, covering, for example, the SADC and IGAD sub-regions, East Asia, and West Asia. It makes sense to establish such additional centers focusing on prevention, but this needs the go-ahead from regional governments, which has not been forthcoming. Seventh, while Chapter VI of the UN Charter is always present, there has been little inclination on the part of member states to draw on it. Eighth, there is a measure of cooperation between the United Nations and regional organizations such as the AU to help head off crises. Ninth, the thematic and country rapporteurs/ representatives of the Human Rights Council (UNHRC) do raise alerts about the risks of human rights violations. And tenth, the UNHRC convenes special sessions on occasion to deal with urgent situations.

Despite all the above, numerous crises, conflicts, gross violations of human rights, and humanitarian disasters occur around the world and it is therefore fair to ask whether debates in the Security Council contribute much, tangibly, to the enhancement of future UN preventive diplomacy. The sad answer to this question may be "Unfortunately, no."[15]

How, then, can UN preventive diplomacy be enhanced in the future— while we await the secretary-general's "platform" to materialize? The practical answer might be to establish more UN sub-regional centers focusing on prevention. Working on the ground discreetly, they can do much to promote confidence-building, assist parties to defuse situations, and to encourage fair-minded practical solutions.

This, to be sure, will require resources. But it is in the interest of the countries concerned and their well-wishers, to make voluntary contributions until such time as regular budget funding can be agreed upon. This could be the direction of travel of the UN peace agenda. The secretary-general is ideally placed to lead this practical surge in UN preventive diplomacy.

UN sub-regional offices for preventive diplomacy

As mentioned, the UN has regional offices dedicated to preventive diplomacy in three sub-regions: the UN Regional Centre for Preventive Diplomacy in Central Asia (UNRCCA), the UN Office for Central Africa (UNOCA), and the UN Office for West Africa and the Sahel (UNOWAS). Historically, the office for West Africa was the first, but it was merged in 2016 into the current office for West Africa and the Sahel.

UNOWAS's mandate, as agreed by the Security Council in December 2016, covers four objectives. First, to monitor political developments in West Africa and the Sahel and carry out good offices and special assignments on behalf of the secretary-general, to assist in peacebuilding, sustaining peace efforts, and enhancing sub-regional capacities for conflict prevention and mediation in the countries of West Africa and the Sahel. Second, to enhance capacities to address cross-border and cross-cutting threats to peace and security in the region, in particular election-related instability and challenges related to security sector reform, transnational organized crime, illicit trafficking, terrorism, and violent extremism (as and when conducive to terrorism). Third, to support the implementation of the UN integrated strategy for the Sahel and the coordination of international and regional engagements in the region. And fourth, to promote good governance and respect for the rule of law, for human rights, and for the mainstreaming of gender into conflict prevention and management initiatives in West Africa and the Sahel.

UNOCA was established in 2011 and covers the 11 member states of the Economic Community of Central African States (ECCAS): Angola, Burundi, Cameroon, Central African Republic, Chad, the Republic of the Congo, the Democratic Republic of the Congo, Equatorial Guinea, Gabon, Rwanda, and Sao Tome and Principe. UNOCA was established essentially to contribute to capacity building in the areas of conflict prevention and peacebuilding in the Central African region. The region has also been grappling with cross-border challenges relating particularly to arms trafficking; piracy and maritime security in the Gulf of Guinea; organized transnational crime; poaching of elephants and illicit traffic of ivory; and the proliferation of armed groups, including the Lord's Resistance Army (LRA) and Boko Haram. The latter movement, while based in Nigeria, is considered a serious threat to various countries of the Central African sub-region, especially Cameroon and Chad.

UNRCCA was established in 2007. It sees its mandate as assisting the five countries of Central Asia—Kazakhstan, Kyrgyzstan, Tajikistan, Turkmenistan, and Uzbekistan—in building their conflict prevention capacities through enhanced dialogue, confidence-building measures, and

18　*The United Nations*

genuine partnership so as to respond to existing threats and emerging challenges in the region. UNRCCA's program of action for 2018–2020, adopted in consultation with the five regional countries, includes five priority areas: promoting prevention among the governments of Central Asia, monitoring and early warning, building partnerships for prevention, strengthening the UN's preventive activities in the region, and encouraging cooperation and interaction between Central Asia and Afghanistan.

The mandates of the three sub-regional offices cover some similar issues and others that are specific to their particular location. It will give an idea of their substantive activities to take them thematically under the headings of fragile states, states in conflict, and post-conflict states. First, in terms of fragile states, Secretary-General Guterres submitted to the Security Council a report in December 2018 on the activities of UNOWAS that year. It stated that the political situation in West Africa and the Sahel remained stable despite significant security challenges, in particular in Burkina Faso, the Niger, and Nigeria, with an increase in the cross-border activities of terrorist groups and a retreat of state authorities from peripheral zones where populations continued to live precariously.

On security trends, they also remained volatile in Burkina Faso, Mali, the Niger, and Nigeria, with repeated attacks against civilians and the military by armed nonstate actors, including terrorist groups, criminal networks, and community-based militias. Burkina Faso faced increased attacks by extremist groups in the east and south of the country, heightening security risks for neighboring countries including Benin, the Niger, and potentially, Togo. There had also been an upswing in intercommunal violence, in particular in the Niger along its western border with Mali. Despite increased military operations, attacks by herdsmen and bandits continued to exacerbate insecurity in Nigeria against the backdrop of several large-scale attacks launched by Boko Haram on the military. Terrorist groups operating in the Sahel appeared to be enhancing coordination, with patterns of attacks indicating a division of labor and close cooperation among groups.

On socio-economic trends, the report stated that the region's economic growth was projected to reach 2.9 percent in 2019. The humanitarian situation in West Africa remained worrying, mainly owing to food insecurity and forced displacements, aggravated by cyclical epidemics and vulnerability to external shocks. Around 24 million people in the region required humanitarian assistance. Furthermore, the overall human rights situation in West Africa and the Sahel remained concerning. Terrorist groups continued to violate international humanitarian and human rights law, with a negative impact on the safety and security of communities. The increasing scope and intensity of clashes between farmers and herders, as well as

The United Nations 19

intercommunal violence, banditry, and cattle rustling, undermined the rights to life, physical integrity, and property of indigenous communities, as well as the right to judicial remedy, as perpetrators continued to act with impunity.

Moving on to states in conflict, while Afghanistan is not formally a member of UNRCCA, it is a neighboring state to its members, and so the office does seek to contribute to preventive diplomacy there. UNRCCA's Programme of Action for 2018–2020 includes "Encouraging cooperation and interaction between Central Asia and Afghanistan."

Building a regional partnership in Afghanistan and Central Asia was the topic of a Security Council meeting in January 2018. Addressing the council, Secretary-General Guterres noted that Central Asian countries bordering Afghanistan are improving their cross-border infrastructure, while security challenges continue to define much of the discussion surrounding the region. The Afghan government's fight against violent extremism, terrorism, and transnational organized crime has implications for the entire region and for the world. Responding to such threats cannot be the responsibility of the Afghan government alone—effective counter-terrorism depends upon regional and multilateral cooperation based firmly on human rights. UNRCCA and the United Nations Assistance Mission in Afghanistan (UNAMA) cooperate closely and continue to seek out new ways to deepen support: with greater regional cooperation and investment, Central Asia and Afghanistan have the potential to become symbols of dialogue, peace, and the promotion of contacts among cultures, religions, and civilizations.[16]

The Kazakh government stated in the meeting that it considers one of the threats facing the region to be the intensification of the activities of terrorist groups, particularly the Islamic State in Iraq and al Sham (ISIS; also known as the Islamic State in Iraq and the Levant, ISIL, Da'esh) in the northern parts of Afghanistan and the potential return of foreign terrorist fighters to their countries of origin, including in Central Asia. Another threat is posed by narcotics production in Afghanistan. The Tajik representative backed up this concern by referring to the activation of radical terrorist groups such as ISIS, the Taliban, the Islamic Movement of Uzbekistan, the Ansarullah Movement, and others in the northern districts of Afghanistan against the backdrop of the significant influx of narcotics, weapons, and human resources.

Similarly, the Turkmen representative noted the role of diplomacy in preventing conflicts, dealing with their root causes, promoting an atmosphere of trust among countries and creating conditions conducive to effective interaction among states in the political, diplomatic, economic, social, environmental, and other spheres, attaching particular importance to the activities of UNRCCA. Over the ten years of its existence, the center

20 *The United Nations*

had provided the governments of Central Asia with a platform for dialogue on the most important regional issues, including the management of shared resources, combating such transnational threats as terrorism, violent extremism, organized crime, drug trafficking, and human trafficking, and making joint efforts to help stabilize the situation in Afghanistan.[17]

Turning lastly to post-conflict states, the secretary-general's 2018 report to the Security Council on UNOWAS provides detailed information on its activities in relation to such countries. His special representative for West Africa and the Sahel continues to support efforts to sustain peace in the region, in collaboration with regional and international partners, by promoting and supporting inclusive national dialogues, human rights, and constitutional and institutional reforms, as well as via transparent, credible, and peaceful elections.

The special representative visited Liberia, encouraging national authorities and civil society to work together to strengthen governance, including in the security sector; and Guinea, for discussions with the government and opposition, encouraging stakeholders to accelerate the implementation of political agreement and to seek consensual solutions to reform of the Electoral Commission. He also continued consultations with key national stakeholders in Nigeria to promote an environment conducive to peaceful general elections in 2019, initiating and participating in a joint pre-electoral mission to Nigeria with ECOWAS and the African Union, during which he consulted with the president, the Office of the Inspector-General, senior military officials, civil society organizations, and other key actors.

A visit was also made to Benin, engaging with government stakeholders regarding preparations for the 2019 legislative elections and ongoing political reforms; and Burkina Faso, Cote d'Ivoire, and the Gambia, focusing on the importance of overcoming challenges to national reconciliation. During meetings in Burkina Faso interlocutors highlighted popular expectations and frustrations arising from economic decline, as well as the fragile security situation of the country. The president of the High Council for Reconciliation and National Unity emphasized the need to re-establish confidence between the population and the authorities.

In the Gambia, the special representative participated in the launch of the Truth, Reconciliation and Reparation Commission. During meetings with the president, he appealed for the commission to adopt a victim-centered approach, with special attention to women, children, and vulnerable groups, and to ensure the protection of victims and witnesses. The discussions also focused on follow-up to the international conference on the national development plan, internal political dynamics, security sector reform, transitional justice, the statelessness of refugee children, and land governance. In Cote d'Ivoire, the special representative encouraged the

The United Nations 21

government to develop a new request for eligibility for funds from the Peacebuilding Fund for 2020.

The special representatives of the secretary-general in charge of the three regional offices brief the Security Council regularly, at its request, on their activities. After such a briefing in January 2018 by the head of UNRCCA, for example, the council reaffirmed the importance of preventive diplomacy in supporting United Nations efforts to assist in the peaceful settlement of disputes and acknowledged the role of the center in assisting the Central Asian states to respond to transnational threats to peace, and to support sustainable development in the region. Council members also welcomed the center's engagement on border management issues and its preparedness to assist the Central Asian states to reduce the potential for violence in border areas.

They also commended the ongoing efforts of UNRCCA to assist the Central Asian states in transboundary water management, and encouraged the center to continue to liaise with the governments of the region and with other parties concerned with issues relevant to preventive diplomacy.[18]

Addressing a conference in Ashgabat in December 2018, the special representative in charge of UNRCCA stated:

> One of the most important things that we do, I believe, is working to build trust among the leaders and peoples of the five countries of the region. This we achieve by creating opportunities for cooperation and people-to-people contacts, not only among high-ranking leaders but also civil servants, civil society, women, youth and others.[19]

The foregoing snapshots of the activities of the three UN sub-regional offices show the multi-faceted nature of their contemporary preventive diplomacy.

UN peace and development advisors

In 2004, the UN Department of Political Affairs (DPA)[20] and UNDP cooperated to create conflict prevention initiatives to operate in the field, via the Joint UNDP-DPA Program on Building National Capacities for Conflict Prevention (Joint Program). The program is aimed at constructing national capacities and supporting conflict prevention initiatives in states undergoing conflict, those with high levels of state fragility, and those undergoing a difficult political transition.

The Joint Program has established the following institutional and procedural initiatives: Peace and Development Advisors (PDAs) to facilitate the building of long-term national capacity, and UN Country Teams

22 *The United Nations*

(UNCT) to create and implement relevant programs; mechanisms and capacities to facilitate collaboration and dialogue; mechanisms to enable the deployment of short-term technical expertise for swifter crisis response; and coordination of UNDP and DPA country engagement. The deployment of PDAs is considered the flagship and the most visible output of the Joint Program. Some 41 of the 45 countries currently supported by the Joint Program host a PDA. They are deployed throughout Africa, Europe, and the Commonwealth of Independent States (CIS), the Asia/Pacific region, Latin America, and among Arab states. PDAs tend to engage in the following functions: the provision of strategic and analytical support to on-the-ground UN resident coordinators in their interactions with high-level officials, civil society, and academia, etc.; supporting the resident coordinator in preparing the UN response to government requests in relation to democratic reform and conflict prevention, etc.; creating and strengthening partnerships with national, regional, and international actors; and the provision of advice on conflict prevention programming and work to strengthen the capacity of UNDP and the UNCT in conducting conflict analysis.

An example of the work of PDAs is found in support for the peace process in Colombia. A PDA was deployed there in 2014 to support the UN role in the emerging peace process. The PDA's responsibilities focused mostly on the four functional areas of the Joint Program rather than in sustained activities to build national capacities for conflict prevention. Tasks included providing support to the resident coordinator in interactions with national stakeholders and the diplomatic community; facilitating UNCT's work on the peace process and preparations for the post-conflict environment; and taking the lead in UN communications activities in support of the peace process.[21]

Human rights

International law, starting with the UN Charter, places several major obligations on states in regard to what are key to prevention—respect for and protection of human rights. See Box 1.2 below for details.

Two things may be said of the role of the United Nations in the prevention of gross violations of human rights: first, most of its activities in this area have an inherently preventive rationale, and, second, faced with situations where gross violations of human rights are threatened, the UN is very rarely able to actually prevent them. We will examine both aspects below, starting with a new UN strategy and plan of action to combat hate speech, launched on June 19, 2019, which has an explicit preventive rationale.

The United Nations 23

Box 1.2 Respect for and protection of human rights as the key to prevention

Respect for and protection of human rights are the key to prevention of violations. In that regard, international law places the following obligations on every government:

1 The United Nations Charter and the Universal Declaration of Human Rights are binding on all governments, which are internationally accountable for upholding them;
2 Following ratification, a human rights treaty must be inserted into national law, whereupon it takes precedence over any conflicting national law or practice;
3 In compliance with the treaty obligation, a country must put into place a national protecting system to ensure compliance with its provisions. Human rights treaty obligations are best implemented under democracy and the rule of law;
4 Only derogations expressly provided for in the treaty may be made—when absolutely necessary—but they must be proportionate to the threat being dealt with, which must have been publicly declared;
5 **Governments have an obligation to take preventive measures against violations of human rights treaty obligations;**
6 The duty to respect means that a good faith effort must be made to comply with the provisions of a human rights treaty in law and in practice. The duty to protect means that the state must act for the prevention of violations of human rights and, if violations do take place, must act to bring them to a stop speedily and provide an appropriate remedy to the victims. The duty to ensure refers to "the duty of the States Parties to organize the governmental apparatus and, in general, all structures through which public power is exercised, so that they are capable of juridically ensuring the free and full enjoyment of human rights";[1]
7 A government has a duty to provide appropriate and adequate redress for violations of human rights;
8 In supervising government reports under a human rights treaty, the aim of the exercise is to show the degree of actual satisfaction of the rights and freedoms in the convention;[2]
9 In considering petitions under a human rights treaty the aim of the exercise is to render justice to the petitioner;
10 In undertaking fact-finding under a human rights treaty, the aim of the exercise is to shed light on the degree of satisfaction of the rights and freedoms in the relevant convention;
11 The principle of equality is fundamental in the implementation of human rights treaty obligations. Equality must be assured in law and in practice; and

24   *The United Nations*

> 12   The principle of justice is the key yardstick in the implementation of human rights treaty obligations. Justice is served by commencing on the side of the petitioner but by being scrupulously fair to all sides.
>
> Source: The author
>
> Notes
> 1 Inter-American Court of Human Rights, Velasquez Rodriguez Case, Judgment, July 29, 1988, Ser. C, No. 4, 1988, para. 165.
> 2 African Commission on Human & Peoples' Rights, "Guidelines for National Periodic Reports," 1989, 49, www.achpr.org/statereportingproceduresandguidelines.

UN strategy and plan of action on hate speech

In the summer of 2019, Secretary-General Guterres launched a UN strategy and plan of action on hate speech. In his foreword, he underscores its preventive rationale. "Hate speech", he wrote, "is a menace to democratic values, social stability, and peace". Tackling hate speech is crucial to deepening progress across the UN agenda by helping to prevent armed conflict, atrocity crimes, terrorism, violence against women, and other serious violations of human rights, as well as to promote peaceful, inclusive, and just societies.

The objectives of the strategy are two-fold: to enhance UN efforts to address root causes and drivers of hate speech, and to enable effective UN responses to the impact of hate speech on societies. The implementation of the strategy is in line with the right to freedom of opinion and expression. The UN supports more speech, not less, as the key means to address hate speech.

The key commitments of the strategy are: to monitor and analyze hate speech; to address root causes, drivers, and actors of hate speech; to engage with and support the victims of hate speech; to use education as a tool for addressing and countering hate speech; to foster peaceful, inclusive, and just societies to address the root causes and drivers of hate speech; to engage in advocacy; and to support member states. The UN hopes, upon request, to provide support to member states in the field of capacity building and policy development to address hate speech. In this regard, the UN aims to convene an international conference—involving national education ministers—on education and prevention with a focus on addressing and countering hate speech.

Presenting the strategy to the UN Economic and Social Council (ECOSOC) on June 18, 2019, the secretary-general noted that, over the past 75 years, hate speech has been a precursor to atrocity crimes, including genocide, from Rwanda to Bosnia to Cambodia. Underscoring the preventive rationale of the strategy, he urged the international community to treat hate speech, like any other malicious act, by condemning it unconditionally, refusing to amplify it, countering it with the truth, and encouraging the perpetrators to change their behavior.

Human rights treaty bodies

Alongside the 1948 Universal Declaration of Human Rights, the two 1966 human rights covenants—the International Covenant on Civil and Political Rights; and International Covenant on Economic, Social and Cultural Rights—are the core of the International Bill of Human Rights that the United Nations resolved to bring about at its inception. Within this core, the Human Rights Committee takes pride of place. For it is this organization, more than any other human rights body in the United Nations, that has given content to the contemporary concept of human rights protection in international law.

In the first place, the committee has shown remarkable foresight in regard to what may be termed the international public order dimensions of protection. The concept of norms of international public order is one that has become famous in international law. The Human Rights Committee's general comment on the legality of the possession and use of nuclear weapons, adopted at the height of the Cold War, was a foundational contribution of the highest order to the contemporary protection concept.

Second, the committee has helped give content to structural dimensions of protection, namely the content of the national protection system that every government is expected to put in place and nurture. The concept of a national protection system in each country is one of the most strategic in the contemporary international law of human rights. It requires that the constitutional, legislative, judicial, educational, institutional, and preventive architecture of a country be in conformity with international human rights law. The committee gives content to the requirements of a national protection system in its Concluding Observations on country reports, its decisions under the Optional Protocol, and in its General Comments.

Third, it has made landmark contributions to the preventive dimensions of protection. In its case law, Concluding Observations on country reports, and General Comments, the committee has required governments to show that they have in place laws, institutions, and policies designed to prevent violations of human rights, especially gross violations. Fourth, the committee has clarified the law on mitigatory and curative protection. Also, in its case law, Concluding Observations, and General Comments, it has called on state parties to act expeditiously for the curtailment of human rights violations the moment they come to the knowledge of a government.

26   *The United Nations*

Fifth, the committee has developed the law on remedial and compensatory protection; its jurisprudence is one of the richest on the topic. Lastly, it has established the legal principle of "contemporaneity" in human rights protection, namely that the law should be interpreted and applied in the light of contemporary circumstances. In this way it has made the law of human rights protection a living law and contributed to the progressive development of the international human rights law.

However, it has to be said that many state parties to the International Covenant on Civil and Political Rights do not actually abide by these standards of protection and prevention, and there is a global crisis when it comes to actual protection. Nevertheless, it is important as a matter of international public law and order that the committee has carefully elaborated this policy framework.

Going beyond the Human Rights Committee, there are nine other human rights treaty bodies operating at the UN, and all contribute to a legislative and policy framework for protection and prevention of gross violations. Three human rights treaties have an explicit preventive purpose: the Convention against Genocide, the Convention against Torture and its Optional Protocol, and the European Convention for the Prevention of Torture. The Optional Protocol to the Convention against Torture provides for a system of visits to prisons and other places of detention where prisoners and detainees are at risk of being tortured and this treaty has the most explicit preventive objectives. However, torture continues to be prevalent in the world. In addition, it could be argued that at their core all human rights treaties have a preventive rationale.

The UN Human Rights Council

The Human Rights Council's mandate authorizes it to contribute, through dialogue and cooperation, toward the prevention of human rights violations and to respond promptly to human rights emergencies. UNHRC is still at the exploratory stage of consideration of the role of prevention, having so far adopted only a few tentative resolutions on the topic. At its request, the Office of High Commissioner for Human Rights has organized expert workshops and round tables on this subject, but it is clear that many governments are not willing to agree to a dynamic preventive role for UNHRC. At the time of writing, the Human Rights Council has designated three experts to lead a series of discussions on how its preventive role might be activated. An NGO, the Universal Rights Group, has been active in encouraging the development of a preventive role for UNHRC but, for the time being, the matter is largely in abeyance, except for the fact that the council sometimes meets in emergency sessions to discuss situations of concern.

The United Nations 27

UNHRC has, on occasion, requested OHCHR to submit sectoral reports on prevention. At the former's request, in March 2011 OHCHR presented to it a report on the human rights aspects of preventable maternal mortality and morbidity. After considering the report the council requested OHCHR to prepare an analytical compilation on good and effective practices to prevent maternal mortality and morbidity.[22] The following month, OHCHR presented a helpful report to the council on good practices in efforts aimed at preventing violence.[23] Next to the human rights treaty bodies, some of the most important UN protection actors are the fact-finders of the council, historically known as the "special procedures," discussed below.

Special procedures of the Human Rights Council

Historically, UN petition procedures have received mixed assessments. Yet, depending on the country concerned, they have sometimes been helpful. During the Cold War, petitions claiming the right to leave one's country that reached the UN from states such as Romania led to marked increases in the numbers of persons allowed to emigrate.[24] Nowadays, petitions reaching the UN are mainly handled by the special procedures, which transmit them to governments for their urgent attention. This sometimes leads to preventive and protective action by the government concerned.

Thematic special procedures contribute to protection through their efforts to clarify the applicable norms. The special rapporteur on human rights and terrorism, for example, has insisted that in the struggle against terrorism, non-derogable human rights norms must be complied with. The work of the special representative on human rights defenders is a good example of efforts for the protection of persons at risk and of preventive actions. Almost all of the special procedures mandate-holders make urgent intercessions in order to help protect people in need.

The Working Group on Enforced and Involuntary Disappearances is a good example of a special procedure engaged in humanitarian intercession. Upon receipt of reliable reports that a person has been made to "disappear" or is at risk of disappearing, it contacts the government concerned with an urgent request for protection. The special procedures' advocacy, urgent intercessions, humanitarian intercessions, and visits on the spot or to neighboring countries can have preventive or mitigatory effects. The activities of the Working Group on Arbitrary Detention are a good example of efforts for redress. Where needed, special procedures mandate-holders frequently condemn gross violations of human rights and this can have a preventive effect. Like country mandate-holders, the reports of thematic mandate-holders document violations for the historical record and for use in any future initiatives for truth and reconciliation, or for justice.

28   *The United Nations*

Like the human rights treaty bodies, UN human rights special procedures are under attack by governments seeking to reduce their effectiveness. The slogan much used to do this is that the UN should engage in cooperation and dialogue when dealing with human rights issues, even when dealing with clear evidence of the commission of gross or criminal violations of human rights. Notwithstanding these adverse political winds, the quest for stronger prevention is ever present, especially on the part of those moved by their conscience in the face of grievous violations of human rights.

The Office of High Commissioner for Human Rights

As is the case for the Human Rights Council, the preventive role of the Office of High Commissioner for Human Rights is, unfortunately, still largely undeveloped. The explanation for this is that governments are, for the most part, not supportive of OHCHR playing such a role and apply various forms of pressure to assert control.

In her annual report to the then Commission on Human Rights in 2000, then High Commissioner Mary Robinson highlighted the importance of the prevention of gross violations of human rights. The quest for the prevention of gross violations of human rights and of conflicts, she wrote, is a defining issue of our times. It should be a matter of the utmost priority that the international community seeks, at the national, regional, and international levels, to develop societies fashioned in the image of the international norms on human rights. The universal implementation of human rights, economic, social, and cultural, as well as civil and political, is the surest preventive strategy and the most effective way of avoiding the emergence of conflict. The report contains chapters offering preventive strategies on a range of topics. Unfortunately, the commission paid no attention to the report and the high commissioner herself did not follow up.

The historical journey of OHCHR since the assumption of its duty by the first high commissioner in 1994 has seen it go through a struggle to become established. This has involved fighting for resources, to provide services to human rights bodies and special procedures mandate-holders, and for the establishment of human rights field offices, the development of programs to help countries strengthen their national human rights structures, the use of the voice of the high commissioner for protection, and, sometimes, the development of a partnership with the Human Rights Council and Security Council.

Since 2000, field offices of the Office of High Commissioner have expanded in many parts of the world, and they do, on occasion, endeavor to help stave off violations of human rights. It would be fair to count the preventive efforts of OHCHR field offices as a development in the right

The United Nations   29

direction. Still, it should place increasing emphasis in the future on preventive strategies—for example, it needs to take on a role of the human rights arm of a "Global Watch" over human security. If OHCHR is to rise to the challenge launched by successive secretaries-general for greater emphasis to be given to prevention, it would need to have a clearer vision when it comes to preventive human rights strategies.

The concept of a Global Watch over human security could help it develop its future role and it would be well advised to project itself as the human rights arm of such a Global Watch. The concept has been around for some three decades now. In a report to the General Assembly in 1987, then UN Secretary-General Pérez de Cuéllar made the case for the establishment and maintenance of a Global Watch over human security. His vision was one in which international security, including disarmament and international law, development and international economic cooperation, social advancement, basic rights and fundamental freedoms, and human well-being would be the broad areas for the future programs of the United Nations.[25]

The report argued for coherent and integrated policies and preventive strategies in the political, security, economic, social, and human rights areas at the national, regional, and international levels. It emphasized the role of human rights protection as a preventive strategy, arguing that respect for basic human rights and for the dignity and worth of the human person as called for in the UN Charter is a fundamental element in the vibrant and productive global society toward which United Nations efforts must continue to be directed. In the future, the main focus of UN human rights activities should be on bringing universal respect for the norms that had been agreed upon. The challenge of promoting respect for human rights was global. The goal of United Nations bodies must be to translate the wide commitment to human rights into an increasingly persuasive means to eliminate abuses wherever they occur.

OHCHR would need to consider ways and means through which the international community would come to look to it as the human rights arm of a comprehensive Global Watch. It is in the nature of the office that one should expect think pieces in which it tries to present the human rights dimensions of new threats and challenges to the international community. In the contemporary world, human rights are affected by eight phenomena: environmental changes, migratory movements, poverty, conflicts, terrorism, gross violations, inequality, and poor governance. It will be crucial to develop preventive strategies in respect of all of these if we are to ever hope to achieve the universal realization of human rights. Each is discussed in turn below.

Environmental changes, whether they are due to natural or human causes, global warming, encroaching deserts, and rising oceans can affect the rights to life and livelihood of large numbers of people. To the extent

30 *The United Nations*

that preventive actions are possible they should certainly be undertaken. But preventive action is also required from a human rights point of view. Environmental mapping and projections and discussion of desirable policy options can help anticipate human rights problems related to mass exoduses, internal displacement, and refugee movements. One should not wait until the problem is upon us before scrambling to deal with it.

When it comes to migratory movements, there are reliable projections that if the warming trend continues and if oceans rise, millions of people will seek to move across frontiers in the quest for life. It will be necessary to think through a human rights regime to plan for, and cope with, such massive changes. The international and normative policy instruments we have at present are nowhere near adequate.

Two-thirds of the world's population lives in extreme poverty. The Millennium Development Goals, which sought to halve world poverty by 2015, were only partially achieved. The SDGs are also faltering in the goal of eliminating hunger by 2030. It is essential, in the future, to bring into the picture the concept of preventable poverty: every country should be expected to map the situation of its poor, identify the extremely poor, and act to prevent extreme poverty to the extent that this can be achieved using already available national resources. The concept of preventable poverty can be buttressed by giving courts and national human rights institutions the competence to adjudicate on situations of gross violations of economic, social, and cultural rights. Some courts, such as the Indian Supreme Court, have developed social action jurisprudence precisely along these lines.

Turning to conflicts, they continue to be distressingly frequent in many parts of the world. The prevention of conflicts, especially in multi-ethnic countries, is closely related to the promotion and protection of human rights, including cultural rights, and especially the rights of composite populations and minorities. Strategies for the prevention of conflicts must be built on the foundations of respect for human rights.

Terrorism also remains a serious global problem, responsible for grievous violations of human rights. The Security Council has called on UN member states to cooperate in combating this scourge, and has called for counter-terrorism efforts to be pursued with respect for human rights. In fact, preventive measures are necessary to safeguard against violations of human rights in the struggle against terrorism. The National Commission on Terrorist Attacks Upon the United States (more commonly known as the 9/11 Commission) called for independent monitoring bodies to safeguard against excesses. That would be a good starting point for preventive measures in the field of human rights.

Gross violations of human rights continue to be rampant in the world. As mentioned earlier, United Nations human rights special procedures, among

The United Nations 31

others, endeavor to document these violations, to take urgent intercessionary action where possible, and to make the case for justice for the victims. However, international efforts in the future need to place the accent increasingly on preventive strategies, beginning with those at the national level to guard against the dangers of gross violations of human rights.

Inequality on grounds of gender, race, social origin, or economic situation is also widespread. It would be interesting to assess how and to what extent strategies pursued to date are contributing to the prevention of discrimination. Educational efforts especially could be decisive in preventing gender or racial discrimination.

Poor governance is without doubt the cause of a great deal of the misery in the world and wreaks havoc on human rights globally. Efforts for the promotion of democracy and the rule of law are meant to help but they have so far seen only partial results. The suggestion has been made that the Human Rights Council should establish a special rapporteurship on the promotion of democratic governance. In addition, efforts to promote democracy and the rule of law should increasingly build in a preventive dimension. The responsibility to protect must also come into the picture here. Through human rights preventive strategies on issues such as the above, future efforts to build the world of the Universal Declaration of Human Rights might help bring us nearer to the mark.

One of the key strategic ideas in contemporary human rights policy is that the human rights movement should place the spotlight on the adequacy and effectiveness of the national protection system of every country. At the end of the day, it is here that human rights violations should be prevented before they take place. The United Nations has focused on this issue for some years now, viewing a national protection system as having six key components: constitutional, legislative, judicial, educational, preventive, and institutional—the last referring to the need for specialized institutions such as national human rights commissions.

The late Sergio Vieira de Mello, in his only annual report submitted to the then Commission on Human Rights, indicated that he would ask governments to submit concise statements of their national protection systems as a basis for an international dialogue. When this author performed the functions of high commissioner after the departure of de Mello to Baghdad he invited and received such concise statements from some three dozen countries. The idea had been to build and publish these submissions over time as a sort of world report on national protection systems. The thinking behind this was to focus international cooperation and dialogue with governments on the need to strengthen national protection systems in all countries.

The Universal Periodic Review instituted following the establishment of the Human Rights Council provides an opportunity for the UN high

32 *The United Nations*

commissioner for human rights, using the national reports submitted by countries, other relevant materials, and the Human Rights Council's observations on the country reports in order to publish a periodic world report on national protection systems, focusing on every state. This, again, would be a dynamic approach to the practice of preventive human rights diplomacy in the future. The high commissioner, in cooperation with national human rights institutions—where they exist—could keep under review the adequacy of national prevention systems designed to head off gross violations of human rights.

In his final "comprehensive" report on the prevention of armed conflict in 2006,[26] prepared at the request of the General Assembly, Secretary-General Kofi Annan argued that prevention was a shared responsibility which does not diminish the primary obligation of member states to exercise their sovereign duties to their citizens and neighbors. In the case of both intra- and interstate armed conflict the key is to equip states and societies to manage their own problems in ways most appropriate to them. He argued for internally driven initiatives for developing local and national capacities for prevention, fostering home-grown, self-sustaining infrastructures for peace. The aim, he explained, should be to develop the capacity in societies to resolve disputes in internally acceptable ways, reaching a wide constellation of actors in government and civil society. External support for such efforts must be informed by an understanding of the countries and societal dynamics concerned.

He stressed the importance of democracy as a universal value, stating that countries prone to armed conflict merit special assistance with respect to democratization. Democratic governance depends both on a legal framework that protects basic human rights and provides a system of checks and balances, and on functioning rule-of-law institutions. It is the absence of precisely these characteristics that lead people to feel that they must resort to violence in order to be heard. Individual governments must find their own path to democracy, but the UN and its partners offer a variety of important services. These include electoral assistance, constitutional assistance, human rights capacity building, support for good governance, anti-corruption initiatives, and reforms in key sectors, including security and judicial.

The UN high commissioner for refugees has, in the past, deployed good offices to help head off problems. High Commissioner Prince Sadruddin Aga Khan, in a course of lectures at the Hague Academy of International Law in 1976, discussed the criteria for action by his office, identifying three criteria. First, the needs to be met and the action to be undertaken should be strictly humanitarian and non-political. Second, there should be a request to the high commissioner from the government(s) directly concerned. Third, the persons for whom the assistance program is to be implemented must qualify as refugees or be in a situation analogous to that of refugees.[27]

The United Nations 33

In discussing the concept of good offices, he noted that beyond the original conception introduced by the General Assembly the institution remained as useful as ever:

> [F]or contingencies and situations on the fringe of the normal activities of the High Commissioner's Office, these may relate more to diplomacy and the role of "intermediary of good will" which the High Commissioner is sometimes called upon to play. For example, discreet approaches are sometimes made by the UNHCR in the hope of easing a situation involving refugees or displaced persons. Similarly, using the tool of "quiet diplomacy" the High Commissioner is often required to ease the tensions that arise inevitably between the country of origin and the country of asylum. His task then consists in depoliticizing refugee situations and putting them into a purely humanitarian context so that they do not continue to be contentious.[28]

Appeals by the high commissioner for refugees, and visits by the high commissioner or senior officials can be, and have been, part of the good offices or preventive diplomacy exercised by UNHCR. A good example of this is the UNHCR appeal in December 1989 on the issue of the Vietnamese boat people in Hong Kong, asking the territory's government not to forcibly return any more boat people until an international meeting the following month that was being convened to consider new approaches to the problem.[29]

Humanitarian agencies have looked to the political and human rights parts of the United Nations to engage in preventive diplomacy to head off humanitarian emergencies.[30] For example, a former UN high commissioner for refugees, serving as special rapporteur of the UN Commission on Human Rights, submitted a report on human rights and mass exoduses in December 1981 in which he advocated for the introduction of an early-warning system leading to expeditious reporting to the UN secretary-general and competent intergovernmental organs for the purpose of timely action. The report also called for the appointment of a UN "special representative for humanitarian questions" whose tasks would be to forewarn, to monitor, to depoliticize humanitarian situations, to carry out those functions which humanitarian agencies could not assume because of institutional or mandate constraints, and to serve as intermediary of goodwill between the concerned parties. In addition, the report encouraged the establishment of a corps of humanitarian observers which, in case of need, could monitor situations and contribute through their presence to a de-escalation of tensions. The corps would facilitate the work of the proposed special representative.[31]

As can be seen from the above, there is considerable scope for improvement in the efforts of the international community to prevent gross violations of

34   *The United Nations*

human rights. The principal problem has been the political objections of governments. With this in mind, the SDGs adopted in 2015, notably SDG 16, have had in view the enhancement of international cooperation in favor of peace, justice, and inclusive and strong societies. How this initiative is faring will be considered next.

SDG 16

Sustainable Development Goal 16 has introduced a new philosophy of prevention grounded in the pursuit of development, peace, justice, and inclusive and strong institutions in all countries. Its main contribution thus far has been to energize civil society organizations ("We the Peoples"), and in giving inspirational and operational content to the concepts of peace, justice, and equitable institutions. It will hopefully move governments to act similarly in the future.

This is of some importance. The UN's Millennium Declaration laid down a set of values for the twenty-first century, including those of democracy, solidarity, the rule of law, and universal respect for human rights. The associated Millennium Development Goals, however, focused more on bread and butter issues and lack an inspirational, human rights dimension. It took some struggle to achieve this, but the inclusion of SDG 16 has given rise to great hopes because, as we shall see in this chapter, NGOs, and some supportive governments, have alerted the international community dramatically to the risks of conflict in particular situations, have spelled out how considerations of justice should contribute to prevention, and have underlined the centrality of inclusive, equitable, and effective national institutions for good governance and the protection of human rights.

Nevertheless, we need to recognize that SDG 16 is no panacea, and its dividends are still largely in the future. In fact, the UN *SDG Report 2019* candidly stated:

> Realizing the goal of peaceful, just and inclusive societies is still a long way off. In recent years, no substantial advances have been made towards ending violence, promoting the rule of law, strengthening institutions at all levels, or increasing access to justice. Millions of people have been deprived of their security, rights and opportunities, while attacks on human rights activists and journalists are holding back development. More countries are ramping up efforts to uncover human rights abuses and designing laws and regulations that foster more open and just societies. But much more work is needed to ensure that these mechanisms are implemented properly.[32]

The United Nations   35

SDG 16 was a compromise between those who wanted stronger provisions for the promotion and protection of human rights based on democracy and the rule of law among the SDGs, and powerful governments opposed to giving a central role to human rights. This tension persists and has influenced the choice of indicators for measuring follow-up of SDG 16. It specifies the following concrete objectives:

16.1: Significantly reduce all forms of violence and related deaths rates everywhere.

16.2: End abuse, exploitation, trafficking and all forms of violence against and torture of children.

16.3: Promote the rule of law at the national level and international levels and ensure equal access to justice for all.

16.4: By 2030, significantly reduce illicit financial and arms flows, strengthen the recovery and return of stolen assets and combat all forms of organized crime.

16.5: Substantially reduce corruption and bribery in all their forms.

16.6: Develop effective, accountable and transparent institutions at all levels.

16.7: Ensure responsive, inclusive, participatory and representative decision-making at all levels.

16.8: Broaden and strengthen the participation of developing countries in the institutions of global governance.

16.9: By 2030, provide legal identity for all, including birth registrations.

16.10: Ensure public access to information and protect fundamental freedoms, in accordance with national legislation and international agreements.

16.a: Strengthen relevant national institutions, including through international cooperation, for building capacity at all levels, in particular in developing countries, to prevent violence and combat terrorism and crime.

16.b: Promote and enforce non-discriminatory laws and policies for sustainable development.

SDG 16 serves as a rallying cause for civil society partners and could turn out to be an important political, intellectual, and normative framework for

36 *The United Nations*

the pursuit of the overarching goals of peace, justice, and equitable institutions. People of goodwill, mobilizing in support of SDG 16, see a major role for preventive approaches and strategies.

Agenda 2030

The UN's Agenda 2030 seeks to advance sustainable development with a view to reinforcing peace and justice on the foundations of respect for universal human rights. Unfortunately, progress is lagging on all five items. Many voices have already been raised, including that of the UN secretary-general, that the Sustainable Development Goals will not be met by 2030 unless there is a redoubling of efforts. Still, on development as such, there is much effort being made.

To the extent that advances in development might lead to justice for some of the world's poor, the justice component might see some progress by the deadline. However, injustices are commonplace in numerous parts of the world, with the incidence of numerous conflicts and with pervasive and shocking violations of human rights. Even though SDG 16 cannot be fully implemented without tackling such violations, there is a numbing silence about them—notwithstanding the courageous efforts of UN human rights fact-finders and the UN high commissioner for human rights.

When it comes to conflict prevention within Agenda 2030, some preventive diplomacy efforts do take place, to the extent possible, within the United Nations and regional organizations. We have seen examples of this earlier in the chapter. But it would be fair to say that, following its launch in September 2015, there has not been any effort to consciously promote the conflict prevention dimension, other than by NGOs. The national reports reviewed in 2019 within the process of the High-Level Political Review, for example, were largely silent on the issue of conflict prevention. The ministerial deliberations in the ECOSOC and General Assembly hardly touched on the issue.

High-level political forum

On September 24 and 25, 2019, heads of state and government gathered at UN Headquarters in New York to follow up and review progress in the implementation of Agenda 2030. This was the first UN summit on the SDGs in the four years since the adoption of the agenda.

In the Introduction to a special *SDG Report 2019* written for the occasion, Secretary-General Antonio Guterres drew attention to the fact that the global landscape for their implementation had generally deteriorated since 2015, hindering the efforts of governments and other partners.

The United Nations 37

Moreover, the commitment to multilateral cooperation, which was central to implementing major global agreements, was under pressure. Conflicts and instability in many parts of the world have intensified, causing untold human suffering, undermining the realization of the SDGs, and even reversing progress already made. With developing countries hosting more than 85 percent of the 68.5 million people forcibly displaced in 2017, pressures on existing support systems have been immense.

In the report chapter devoted to SDG 16, it was stated that advances in ending violence, promoting the rule of law, strengthening institutions, and increasing access to justice have been uneven and continue to deprive millions of their security, rights, and opportunities, and undermine the delivery of public services and broader economic development. Attacks on civil society are also holding back development progress. Renewed efforts were claimed to be essential to move to the achievement of SDG 16.

In discussing progress or lack thereof in relation to Goal 16, the report noted that the number of intentional homicides per 100,000 people have increased slightly, with various forms of violence against children persisting, and a modest increase in the detection of victims of trafficking. The share of unsentenced detainees in the overall prison population has remained largely constant at 30 percent, the killing of human rights defenders, journalists, and trade unionists is on the rise, and birth registrations average just 73 percent globally. It argued that the pace of progress on establishing national human rights institutions compliant with the Paris Principles needed to be accelerated—in 2018, only 39 percent of countries had such an institution. At this rate, by 2030 only 54 percent of all countries will have a compliant institution. The commitment to multilateral cooperation, so central to implementing global agreements, is under immense pressure.

Neither the General Assembly nor the Security Council has deliberated on what more could be done to advance conflict prevention within the framework of SDG 16. As far as is known, neither the secretary-general nor the UN Department of Political and Peacebuilding Affairs (DPPA) has approached the principal regional and sub-regional organizations to ask them to re-double their efforts for conflict prevention as part of their contribution to the implementation of SDG 16. There is also no evidence that any of the regional organizations with peace and security mandates discussed in this book (the AU, ASEAN, ECOWAS, IGAD, OAS, OSCE, or SADC) has deliberated upon how to bolster contributions to conflict prevention as part of their contributions to the implementation of SDG 16.

But for the efforts of NGOs such as the Fund for Peace, the conflict prevention part of the Agenda 2030 has so far been mostly overlooked. This is unfortunate: somewhere within the UN, someone should feel a sense of

38 *The United Nations*

responsibility to integrate the conflict prevention dimension as an integral part of the process of implementing SDG 16. There are numerous practical ways of going about this task: one place to start could be to promote grassroots campaigns for peace in different parts of the world. The encouragement of national arrangements for conflict prevention would be another example. UN organs such as the General Assembly, the Security Council, ECOSOC, the Human Rights Council, and the Peacebuilding Commission could adopt policy statements on the salience of conflict prevention for the implementation of SDG 16. The secretary-general could also consider designating a special envoy for the implementation of Goal 16 who could contribute to highlighting the centrality of efforts for conflict prevention. Such an envoy might even contribute to the preparation of a "special summit of the General Assembly on conflict prevention and preventive diplomacy."

Conclusion

This chapter has shown that the world is facing an existential crisis as it has never before in recorded human history. Climate change and weapons of mass destruction could destroy civilization, humanity, and the earth. This situation calls for bold new initiatives and new diplomacy.

The IPCC has engaged in spectacular leadership and diplomacy to help save the planet and humanity, and the UN secretary-general and his special envoy have taken the leadership on climate change. In a later chapter the extraordinary leadership of a teenage global leader, Greta Thunberg, is discussed. Hers has not only been advocacy, but preventive diplomacy: addressing influential meetings, national parliaments, and UN gatherings to plead the case for humanity to change course. It is preventive diplomacy of a new kind, people's preventive diplomacy in the face of the threats facing the Earth and humankind.

We have also seen dramatic new efforts by the UN regional centers for preventive diplomacy to help contain crises and turn them around. They deal with root causes as well as manifestations of crises. The leaders of these centers engage in imaginative diplomacy to help head off crises or to contain them to the extent possible. Contemporary preventive diplomacy partakes of not only prevention, but peacemaking, peacebuilding, and peacekeeping. Whatever works to prevent, contain, or mitigate a crisis is tried.

One can see imaginative new approaches such as the deployment of UN peace and development advisers, the facilitation of local mediators, and the contribution of UN crisis bureaus to help build national infrastructures for crisis prevention in the aftermath of natural or human-made disasters. It would be fair to say that the UN is mobilizing everything it can in the effort to prevent and mitigate conflicts and violence.

The United Nations 39

When it comes to the prevention of gross violations of human rights, the underlying rationale of UN human rights programs is preventive: to encourage governments to apply international human rights standards so as to foster justice and thereby avoid grievances, conflicts, and violations of human rights. Unfortunately, although governments subscribe to UN human rights norms on paper, they violate them openly inside their countries and resist a role for the UN in calling them to account. The prevention of gross violations of human rights remains a daunting challenge.

Nevertheless, the Office of High Commissioner for Human Rights must embark on a course of serving as the human rights arm of a de-facto "Global Watch Over Human Security." OHCHR can perform this role through its research program and the publication of reports that serve as think-pieces for the international community in alerting it to the human rights dimensions of existing and emergent global problems. There is a role waiting to be played here and OHCHR should step up to the plate.

We have seen that SDG 16 seeks to bring together efforts for development, peace, justice, and equitable institutions. At its core, it has a preventive mission. Unfortunately, while discussions have focused on the development aspects of the SDGs, very little has been done on Goal 16's other components. NGOs have mobilized and produced useful reports: for example, the Fund for Peace produces an annual report alerting the international community to situations of danger. And NGOs have highlighted the centrality of justice for conflict prevention but, in a world where so many governments are undemocratic and commit grievous violations of human rights on their own people, states have not been willing to activate the justice dimension of SDG 16.

So, in summary, unprecedented times call for innovative leadership and diplomacy. The UN is doing its utmost to spearhead international action. But the Achilles heel, when it comes to peace, justice, human rights, conflict prevention, and equitable national institutions, remains the lack of democracy in the majority of countries in the world. Is humanity, then, hurtling to disaster? Greta Thunberg put it well:

> I want you to panic. I want you to feel the fear I feel every day. And then I want you to act. I want you to act as you would in a crisis. I want you to act as if our house is on fire. Because it is.[33]

Notes

1 IPCC, *Special Report on Climate Change, Desertification, Land Degradation, Sustainable Land Management, Food Security, and Greenhouse Gas Fluxes in Terrestrial Ecosystems* (New York: United Nations, 2019).
2 Christopher Flavelle, "Warming Planet Threatens Food Supply, a UN Report Warns," *New York Times International Edition*, August 9, 2019. See, similarly,

40 *The United Nations*

a front-page story by Somini Sengupta and Weiyi Cai, "A Quarter of Humanity Faces Looming Water Crises," *New York Times*, August 8, 2019.

3 IPCC, *Special Report on the Ocean and Cryosphere in a Changing Climate*, (New York: United Nations, Sep 2019). Available at www.ipcc.ch/srocc/.

4 Camilla Hodgson and Leslie Hook, "Sea Level Rises Faster as Polar Ice Melts, Warns UN Report," *Financial Times*, September 25, 2019.

5 *The Economist*, "How to Think about Global Warming and War: They Are Linked—and That Is Worrying," May 23, 2019, 15–16, Available at www. economist.com/leaders/2019/05/23/how-to-think-about-global-warming-and-war.

6 See UN, Climate Action Summit 2019: "The Climate Crisis—A Race We Can Win." Available at www.un.org/en/un75/climate-crisis-race-we-can-win.

7 See UN Climate Action, interview with Special Envoy Luis Alfonso de Alba. Available at www.un.org/en/climatechange/special-envoy-alba-interview. shtml.

8 *UN News*, "Action Not Words: What Was Promised at the UN's Landmark Climate Summit?" September 23, 2019.

9 A full list of the initiatives announced during the Climate Action Summit can be found at: www.un.org/en/climatechange/press-materials.shtml.

10 See on this, Security Council Report, "In Hindsight: The Security Council and Climate Change—An Ambivalent Relationship," August 2017 Monthly Forecast.

11 *UN News*, "UN Chief Launches New Disarmament Agenda 'to Secure Our World and Our Future,'" May 24, 2018.

12 UNODA, "The Secretary-General's Agenda for Disarmament," fact sheet, January 2019.

13 Ibid.

14 See on this, UN Department of Political Affairs 2018, "United Nations Conflict Prevention and Preventive Diplomacy in Action: An Overview of the Role, Approach and Tools of the United Nations and its Partners in Preventing Violent Conflict,". Available at https://dppa.un.org/sites/default/files/booklet_200618_fin_scrn.pdf.

15 The latest Security Council debate on the topic, largely an exhortative one, took place on October 7, 2019.

16 UN Security Council, 8162nd Meeting, UN doc. S/PV. 8162, January 19, 2018, 3–4.

17 Ibid., 30–31.

18 UNRCCA, "Security Council Press Statement on UNRCCA," January 26, 2018, https://unrcca.unmissions.org/security-council-press-statement-unrcca. This referred to a Security meeting on January 22, 2018.

19 UNRCCA, "Statement by SRSG Natalya Gherman at the Conference 'Importance of the Great Silk Road: Present and Future Development,'" December 6, 2018, 2.

20 Note that, in January 2019, the Department of Political Affairs and the Department of Peacekeeping Operations (DPKO) merged to become the Department of Political and Peacebuilding Affairs (DPPA).

21 UNDPA, "Lessons Learned Study: Peace and Development Advisors: Building National Capacities for Conflict Prevention," January 18, 2017, 6, 13.

22 See UN General Assembly, "Report of the United Nations High Commissioner for Human Rights on the Question of the Realization in All Countries of

The United Nations 41

Economic, Social and Cultural Rights," Human Rights Council, Seventeenth Session, UN doc. A/HRC/17/24, March 21, 2011, para. 5.

23 UN General Assembly, "Report of the Office of the United Nations High Commissioner for Human Rights on Good Practices in Efforts Aimed at Preventing Violence Against Women," Human Rights Council, Seventeenth Session, UN doc. A/HRC/17/23, April 19, 2011.

24 Author interview with Jakob Moller, Chief of the Petitions Unit 1970–1996, Geneva, January 15, 2008.

25 UN Secretary-General, "Preparation for the Medium-Term Plan, Note by the Secretary-General. Enclosure: Some Perspectives on the Work of the United Nations in the 1990s," UN doc. A/42/512, September 2, 1987, 2.

26 UN General Assembly, "Progress Report on the Prevention of Armed Conflict: Report of the Secretary-General," UN doc. A/60/891, July 18, 2006.

27 See UNHCR, "Lectures by Prince Sadruddin Aga Khan, United Nations High Commissioner for Refugees, on Legal Problems Relating to Refugees and Displaced Persons, Given at the Hague Academy of International Law, 4–6 August 1976." Available at http://repository.forcedmigration.org/pdf/?pid=fmo:3356.

28 Ibid.

29 New York Times, "UN Asks Hong Kong to Delay Deportations," December 17, 1989.

30 See, for example, International Institute of Humanitarian Law, Round Table on Pre-Flow Aspects of the Refugee Phenomenon, San Remo, April 27–30, 1982.

31 United Nations Economic and Social Council, "Question of the Violation of Human Rights and Fundamental Freedoms in Any Part of the World, with Particular Reference to Colonial and Other Dependent Countries and Territories: Study on Human Rights and Massive Exoduses," report to the Commission on Human Rights by Prince Sadruddin Aga Khan, UN doc. E/CN.4/1503, December 31, 1981.

32 UN, The Sustainable Development Goals Report 2019 (New York, 2019), 32. Available at https://unstats.un.org/sdgs/report/2019/The-Sustainable-Development-Goals-Report-2019.pdf.

33 Greta Thunberg, No One Is Too Small to Make a Difference (London: Penguin, 2019), 24.

2 Africa
The AU and sub-regional organizations

- The African Union
- The Economic Community of West African States
- The Intergovernmental Authority on Development
- The Southern African Development Community
- Conclusion

Preventive diplomacy by the African Union and its partner organizations the Economic Community of West African States, the Intergovernmental Authority on Development, and the Southern African Development Community has been full of heart, inventive, persistent, and challenging. While there have undoubtedly been successes, such as those following efforts of the AU Panel of the Wise, there have also been frustrations. This is probably explained by the difficult historical, geographical, economic, social, and political circumstances in many countries.

As Jeffrey Sachs has written, much of tropical Africa is landlocked; in fact, with 16 countries, Africa has the highest number of landlocked countries in the world. At independence "many parts of Africa were so poor that the most basic infrastructure—roads, power, water, and sanitation did not even exist." Effectively, Africa was caught in a "poverty trap."[1] This is the difficult terrain in which African efforts for preventive diplomacy have to operate. In discussing these challenges this chapter analyzes in detail efforts by the AU before moving on to explore initiatives by three of the region's most significant other intergovernmental organizations: ECOWAS, IGAD, and SADC.

The African Union

The AU has a broad range of policies and programs whose aims are fundamentally preventive. The AU coordinates the positions of its members on climate change, has an ambitious program on weapons of mass destruction and on the reduction of great numbers of small arms, does a great deal to help prevent and manage conflicts, has a human rights commission that has put down useful building blocks for prevention and protection, and supports the implementation of SDG 16 on peace, justice, and strong institutions. We look at each of these topics in turn in this chapter incorporating, where applicable, the efforts of the sub-regional African organizations. Unfortunately, as in the case with the UN, African organizations continue to be constricted by their own governments, some recalcitrant, many undemocratic and oppressive.

Climate change

The AU's work on environment, climate change, water, land, and natural resources aims at advancing Africa's Climate Change Agenda, including supporting the continent's negotiations on climate change at the global level, and advancing the African Common Position on Climate Change and the formulation of an African Climate Change Strategy. The AU is also looking to improve the continent's exploitation of earth observation technologies through the implementation of the Monitoring for Environment and Security in Africa (MESA) program. It is also working on operationalizing the program on Climate for Development in Africa (ClimDEV-Africa).

Of some importance, the AU is also attempting to implement the Green Wall for the Sahara and Sahel Initiative (GGWSSI) as part of efforts to combat land degradation and desertification; and to advance the African Water and Sanitation Agenda, particularly the Sharm El-Sheikh Commitments on Water and Sanitation, while also supporting the Water Basin Initiatives. Furthermore, it is facilitating the implementation of the African Strategy on Meteorology (Weather and Climate Services) to enhance weather and climate service delivery for sustainable development, and the implementation of the Africa Regional Strategy on Disaster Risk Reduction (DRR), and its Programme of Action in line with the Hyogo Framework for Action.[2]

Despite these initiatives, the need for more mobilized AU preventive diplomacy on climate change was highlighted in a study by Florian Krampe and Vane Moran Aminga, published by the Stockholm International Peace Research Institute (SIPRI) on February 7, 2019. It pointed out that while Africa is responsible for a mere 4 percent of global CO_2 emissions, no continent was so affected by the double burden of climate change and political fragility. Globally, 57 percent of the countries facing the highest double burden of climate exposure and political fragility risks were located in sub-Saharan Africa. African societies, moreover, faced

44 *Africa*

socioeconomic and political challenges, such as endemic poverty, weak and corrupt governance structures, protracted conflicts, demographic pressures, and urbanization.

The authors of the study counseled that responding to climate-related security challenges required an integrated approach that combined knowledge of climate risks with the social and political realities of the region. Being the continent most vulnerable to climate change—inextricably linked to the continent's peace and security—Africa was in need of a clear climate security strategy and strategic leadership.

Part of this, according to the study's authors, should be the appointment of a special envoy on climate change and security who could help widen the understanding of climate-related security risks within the AU. Nevertheless, a special envoy alone would not be enough. African heads of state must take ownership and lead the continent's response to climate-related security risks:

> Cooperation among AU Member States with a Special Envoy for Climate Change and Security will be an opportunity to climate-proof the AU's peace and security architecture, address the root causes of migration and forced displacement, and as such become a catalyst to facilitate the AU's ambitious Agenda 2063.[3]

In short, there is considerable room to improve climate change preventive diplomacy in Africa.

Weapons of mass destruction

The AU common defense policy has identified weapons of mass destruction (WMDs) as a common threat facing all member states that should be addressed in a collective manner. Consequently, states on the continent have agreed the African Nuclear-Weapons-Free Zone Treaty (Pelindaba Treaty), which entered into force in 2009. An African Commission on Nuclear Energy (AFONE) works for its implementation.

The AU contributes to WMD disarmament and non-proliferation by supporting the ratification and implementation of regional and global instruments, including through developing the required human and technical capacities of member states while ensuring that they benefit fully from the peaceful application of related sciences and technologies for socioeconomic development.

The AU secretariat has also initiated work on a model law on chemical, biological, radiological, and nuclear security. It is intended to assist member states with both common and civil law systems in setting up legislation, in full compliance with the regional and international instruments, to strengthen national controls and prevent access and acquisition by criminals and terrorists. It is being tailored to the African context and will serve as a working tool to understand the full scope of obligations, and to assess and address the gaps in domestic legislation.

In addition, an AU program on Disarmament, Demobilization and Reintegration (DDR) was established in 2012 to provide political, technical, and operational support to member states in implementing DDR, to generate and manage knowledge on DDR, and to provide a continental platform for African dialogue on the subject. The program derives its strength from the key partnerships developed with a range of actors, including the World Bank, the United Nations, and sub-regional organizations. It promotes the concept of African ownership over DDR processes and considers national governments as holding primary responsibility for implementation of relevant programs.

The AU has furthermore elaborated a Master Roadmap of Practical Steps to Silence the Guns in Africa, which, among other things, strives to control the proliferation of WMDs. It works on controlling small arms and light weapons (SALW) as well as dealing with land mines. It promotes security sector reform (SSR) and has a program on disarmament, demobilization and reintegration. The organization also has a Post-Conflict Reconstruction and Development Policy as well as a common defense policy.[4]

In attempting to implement the "Master Road Map," and its Silencing the Guns Continental Plan of Action, the AU has organized workshops to develop and validate the West Africa and East Africa chapters of the plan.

The initiative on controlling SALW recognizes that they constitute a serious threat to safety, security, and stability in Africa. In recent years, arms diversion and trafficking have aggravated violent conflicts on the continent, have fueled terrorism, and have enabled a range of human rights and humanitarian violations. The flow of weapons into conflict zones can intensify violence, remove incentives for reconciliation, and undermine the AU's conflict management and resolution efforts.

Outside the immediate context of armed conflict, illicit small arms have also aggravated inter-communal conflict and competition over natural resources, and have facilitated a range of criminal activities in urban settings. In response, in 2013 the AU adopted an Action Plan on the Control of Illicit Proliferation, Circulation and Trafficking of SALW.

Four years later, it adopted the AU Ammunition Safety Management Initiative to assist member states in preventing diversion of ammunition and accidental explosions, which often have serious human and financial costs. Support to member states is provided upon request and in close collaboration with implementing partners, including the UN and the Geneva

46 *Africa*

Center for Humanitarian Demining (GICHD). AU Peace Support Operations (PSOs), by virtue of their mandates, have responsibility for handling significant amounts of recovered weapons and ammunition. The AU has also conducted the first-ever continental mapping study on illicit arms flows. The study was presented to its Peace and Security Council in 2019.

Another important issue is mines and explosive remnants of war (ERW), which continue to threaten death and injury long after conflict is over. Their presence obstructs emergency assistance, impedes the free movement of people and trade, and limits the amount of land that can be used for agriculture and development projects. On this issue, the AU has organized meetings to discuss options for improving improvised explosive device (IED) mitigation approaches, including standardization, inter-operability, coordination platforms, and political and material support needs.

The aim of the AU security sector reform program is to assist member states to formulate and reorient the policies, structures, and capacities of institutions and groups engaged in the security sector, in order to make them more effective, efficient, and responsive to democratic control. The program is guided by the AU Policy Framework on Security Sector Reform, adopted in January 2013. Within this framework, the Defense and Security Division of the AU Commission's Peace and Security Department provides direct technical assistance to member states and works with regional economic communities to promote coherent and effective SSR approaches at the sub-regional level. The Defense and Security Division also provides capacity-building support through tailored training activities and the production of operational guidelines.

Conflicts and violence

The AU is faced with repeated, persistent, and complex conflicts on the continent, in response to which it engages in crisis management while developing an elaborate, multi-pronged strategy for the long-term prevention of conflicts.

The Protocol to the Charter of the African Union established a Peace and Security Council consisting of representatives of ten member states. The council's objectives are to promote and encourage democratic practices, good governance and the rule of law, protect human rights and fundamental freedoms, respect for the sanctity of human life and international humanitarian law, as part of efforts toward preventing conflict.[5] The protocol establishes the AU's right to intervene in a member state if the organization's assembly agrees that there is the threat of commission of a mass atrocity crime—that is, war crimes, genocide, or crimes against humanity.[6] The council can recommend intervention in a member state to the assembly.

Africa 47

The AU commissioner for peace and security supervises a Conflict Prevention and Early Warning Division; a Crisis Management and Post-Conflict Reconstruction Division; a Peace Support Operations Division; a Defense and Security Division; an African Centre for the Study and Research on Terrorism; the AU Mechanism for Police Cooperation; and the African Commission on Nuclear Energy. The commissioner and the secretariat of the Peace and Security Council also cooperate closely with regional economic communities and regional mechanisms for conflict prevention, management, and resolution. Advocacy efforts are targeted, among others, at fostering the role of women in peace and development.

Institutionally, the council, supported by regional and sub-regional organizations, attempts to provide alerts about potential conflicts, to help head them off, and to mediate and conciliate them. On the peacekeeping front, the AU has been working on an African Standby Force. On the cooperation front, the AU and United Nations have an active plan of cooperation to help prevent conflicts on the continent.

The African Union Panel of the Wise is one of the key pillars of the organization's peace and security architecture. It consists of five highly respected personalities from various segments of society who have made outstanding contributions to the cause of peace, security, and development on the continent. Panel members serve for a term of three years, renewable once. The current membership includes former president of Liberia Ellen Johnson Sirleaf.

The panel, on its own initiative or at the request of the AU Peace and Security Council, undertakes action to support the AU's conflict prevention work. The panel meets at least three times annually to deliberate on its work program and to identify situations to visit. It organizes annual workshops on conflict prevention and management. At its first meeting, on December 18, 2007, panel members agreed to undertake regular consultations with experts, academics, and civil society on emerging threats to peace and security through the yearly production of thematic "horizon-scanning" reports aimed at enhancing their ability to anticipate and identify new conflict situations requiring their and the AU's attention. Through this process, members have produced four thematic reports: "Election-Related Disputes and Political Violence"; "Peace, Justice and Reconciliation in Africa"; "Mitigating Vulnerabilities of Women and Children in Armed Conflicts"; and "Strengthening Political Governance for Peace, Security and Stability in Africa."

The panel has sought to develop close relations with other institutions. For example, in May 2013 it launched the Pan-African Network of the Wise (PanWise); and recently initiated the establishment of "FemWise Africa" as a subsidiary body of the Panel. The latter focuses on strengthening the role of

48 *Africa*

women in conflict prevention and mediation efforts by providing a platform for strategic advocacy, capacity building, and networking aimed at enhancing the involvement of women in preventive diplomacy in Africa. To give an idea of how the panel functions, I will describe some of its specific preventive diplomacy efforts. During its mission to the Central African Republic (CAR) in 2007, then undergoing a difficult situation, panel members assessed the current political conditions and the preparations underway for the convening of an inclusive political dialogue. The panel conducted consultations with national political parties, trade unions, civil society organizations, and members of the diplomatic community. After this it compiled a report, presented to the president of CAR, with a recommendation for a national dialogue to be convened in the country. The panel's work has been argued to have helped steer the country on a path of constructive reforms.

The situations in Egypt, Libya, and Tunisia took center stage in the panel's deliberations in May 2011, during the Arab Spring. It was also deeply involved in the Democratic Republic of the Congo for a number of years as it deployed efforts in support of free and fair elections. In January 2012 the panel undertook several pre-election missions to Senegal which contributed to the resolution of the country's political and electoral standoff, marked by violent demonstrations in the capital against the incumbent president's attempt to run for a third term.

The panel also visited Kenya in January 2013 on a pre-election assessment mission ahead of the March 2013 general election. It consulted with a variety of stakeholders with the aim of supporting free and fair elections, as well as to launch the AU's long-term elections observation mission to the country.

The concept of the Panel of the Wise has proved of value, with the panel itself undoubtedly making crucial contributions to the stability of various countries on the continent, particularly in the context of elections-related disputes and political violence. Its deployment of preventive diplomacy has been of great value so far.

AU preventive diplomacy is deployed in many other ways in the processes of conflict prevention, peacemaking, and peacekeeping. For example, in 2019 AU efforts, along with those of the government of Ethiopia, helped defuse the dangerous situation in the Sudan and helped negotiate a political road map among the various factions.

Human rights

The AU has an African Commission on Human and Peoples' Rights and an African Court on Human Rights. These have made modest contributions to the prevention of gross violations of human rights on the continent. We

Africa 49

shall look at some of their jurisprudence later in this section. However, we wish to first highlight an area of human rights protection directly relevant to conflict prevention and preventive diplomacy that has so far been almost totally neglected in Africa, namely the protection of minorities.

The protection of minorities in Africa is a subject practically untouched in the literature or in African policy documents, even though it involves one of the core causes of conflicts and of gross violations of human rights throughout the continent. Sub-Saharan Africa has the greatest concentration of minorities at risk of any region in the world, 74 groups and more than 42 percent of the regional population.[7]

Groups are in danger in 29 out of the 36 countries in the sub-Saharan region having a population of more than one million. Objective cultural differences between dominant groups and minorities are smaller in sub-Saharan Africa, on average, than in all other regions of the world. Thus, cultural differences do not discourage the formation of multi-ethnic coalitions in most countries and it is the dynamics of these coalitions rather than the presence of cultural differences that most effectively explain the persistence of large numbers of minorities in the region.

The topic of minority protection in Africa is one that deserves close attention in the future. Habits of cooperation in the area are needed nationally, regionally, and sub-regionally. The drafting and adoption of an AU declaration on the protection of minorities would provide a good base from which to proceed. The establishment of a post of AU high commissioner on national minorities would also be a good step for the protection of human and minorities rights and the prevention of conflicts in the continent.

The African Commission on Human and Peoples' Rights took a dynamic position on the protection of the rights of an endangered group in the Endorois case, which involved a group whose lands were at risk of being taken over without their agreement. The commission held that they were being denied, among other things, their right to development.

The commission has taken a firm position on the primacy of international human rights law over national law. In a case involving restrictions on freedom of expression under national law, it underlined that governments should avoid restricting rights, and take special care with regard to those rights protected by constitutional or international human rights law. No situation justified the wholesale violation of human rights. According to the African Charter on Human and Peoples' Rights, dissemination of opinions may be restricted by law. However, this does not mean that national law can set aside the right to express and disseminate one's opinions:

> To allow national law to have precedence over the international law of the Charter would defeat the purpose of the rights and freedoms

50 *Africa*

enshrined in the Charter. International human rights standards must always prevail over contradictory national law. Any limitation on the rights of the Charter must be in conformity with the provisions of the Charter.[8]

On the national responsibility to protect human rights, the commission stated in the case of *Commission National des droits de l'homme et des libertes v. Chad* that if a state neglects to ensure the rights guaranteed in the African Charter it can constitute a violation, even if the government is not the immediate cause of the violation.[9] The commission determined that there had been "serious and massive violations of human rights in Chad."

In a case involving Nigeria, the commission found the act of the Nigerian government in nullifying the domestic effect of the African Charter constituted an affront to the charter.[10]

SDG 16

The African Union has recognized that there is a strong link between the UN's Agenda 2030 and the AU's Agenda 2063 for Africa. This connection stems from the latter's first aspiration: "We want a prosperous Africa based on inclusive growth and sustainable development." The African Union is working on the definition of specific needs regarding SDG 16, and in defining how existing mechanisms such as the African Peer Review Mechanism (APRM), can provide in-depth analysis of country-specific targets under Goal 16. The AU has also highlighted a local approach to addressing challenges: in collaboration with the United Nations Economic Commission for Africa (UNECA) and the African Development Bank, it made an assessments of the specific priorities in the region, in order to make an efficient use of available resources to secure concrete advances toward SDG 16.[11] See Box 2.1 below for a broader overview of recent cooperation and coordination between the UN and AU on prevention-related activities.

The Economic Community of West African States

Moving on to other regional organizations, the ECOWAS Conflict Prevention Framework (ECPF) was enacted by the organization's Mediation and Security Council in January 2008, and adopted in its efforts to strengthen human security in West Africa. Achieving this objective requires effective and durable cooperative interventions to prevent or de-escalate violence within and between states, and to resolve conflicts in a peaceful manner, while supporting peacebuilding in post-conflict environments.

Africa 51

Box 2.1 Cooperation between the African Union and the United Nations

African Cooperation on Peace "Increasingly Strong,"
Security Council Told

African countries are building increasingly strong partnerships for advancing peace and security, as well as inclusive sustainable development across the continent, the Security Council heard on Thursday [September 26, 2019], during a briefing by the UN Secretary-General's Chef de Cabinet, Maria Luiza Ribeiro Viotti.

Ms Viotti recognized the African Union and Member States' success in achieving important milestones in their pursuit for higher effectiveness, self-reliance and cooperation, and welcomed the work of the African Union Mediation Support Unit and the FemWise Network of African Women in Conflict Prevention and Mediation, which are, she said, "boosting capacity to defuse crises and making such efforts more inclusive."

Progress evident at regional and country level

Ms. Viotti went on to outline some of the progress being made in certain African countries, such as the peace talks, led by the African Union, in the Central African Republic, which led [to] a Political Agreement which is being overseen by the UN; the signing of a Constitutional Declaration in Sudan, which has allowed for the establishment of a civilian-led government, following efforts led by Ethiopia and the African Union (AU), with UN support; and free and fair elections in Madagascar, supported by the Southern African Development Community, the African Union, and UN.

Cooperation between the UN, African Union and other partners in the area of elections is growing, said Ms Viotti, citing visits organized by the UN Office for West Africa to several countries, ahead of legislative or presidential elections, over the last two years.

The UN and AU, she continued, are cooperating closely to ensure that the voices of women and youth are integral to peace processes, and both organizations have youth envoys and strategies, acting as advocates and agents of change.

More effective support needed from international community

Despite the many examples of progress, Ms Viotti declared that the international community needs to do much more to support African efforts. For example, more predictable, flexible and sustainable financing for African Union-led peace support operations is needed; more political will and resources for peacebuilding and sustaining peace efforts; and active support for the AU initiative on Silencing the Guns …

52 Africa

> "Building partnerships and harnessing their power requires long-term vision and commitment," Ms. Viotti told the Security Council, adding that the Secretary-General is looking forward to "even greater partnership and collaboration, enabling the African Union to achieve its 2063 vision of equitable, people-centred transformation and lasting peace and security."
>
> Source: UN News, "African Cooperation on Peace 'Increasingly Strong', Security Council Told," September 26, 2019

The need for preventive diplomacy within West Africa has arisen out of numerous political, military, and humanitarian crises. ECOWAS leaders have been compelled to intervene in member states to avert imminent political crises, to manage conflicts which have become violent from escalating further, and to ensure that post-conflict peacebuilding processes are sustained. Some of these initiatives have been undertaken by local, regional, and international actors, occasioning the need for, and the enhancement of, coordination and synergy between the mediation efforts of national and local actors on the one hand, and regional processes on the other.

The framework's "Preventive Diplomacy Component" therefore aims at defusing tensions and ensuring the peaceful resolution of disputes within and between member states by means of good offices, mediation, conciliation, and facilitation based on dialogue, mediation, and arbitration. Usually applied in the face of imminent crisis, preventive diplomacy is applicable in the management, resolution, and peacebuilding phases of conflict. Linked to transforming the region from "an ECOWAS of states" to "an ECOWAS of peoples," the component derives its mandate from the 1999 Protocol Relating to the Mechanism for Conflict Prevention, Management, Resolution, Peacekeeping and Security; the 2001 Supplementary Protocol on Democracy and Good Governance; the ECOWAS Conflict Prevention Framework; and the Monrovia Declaration, adopted at the ECOWAS international conference in 2010. The Component also fits into Goal Three of ECOWAS' Community Strategic Framework 2016–2020, which has the purpose of deepening the process of political cohesion and participation, with the strategic objective of ensuring peace, security, and good governance.[12]

ECOWAS also has a Council of the Wise, which has interceded in conflicts in Liberia, Sierra Leone, Niger, Guinea, Guinea-Bissau, and Togo.[13] Related initiatives have been taken by other regional organizations. The Community of Sahel-Saharan States (CEN-SAD) has a "permanent high-level

Africa 53

mediator for peace and security," who has been deployed in Chad, Mali, Niger, and the Central African Republic. The Common Market for Eastern and Southern Africa (COMESA) also plans to establish a "Committee of Elders" as part of its preventive diplomacy strategy. IGAD has been interested in establishing a mediation support unit while the Economic Community of Central African States has its eyes on a "Council of Eminent Persons" as part of its Conflict Prevention, Management and Resolution Protocol.[14]

The Intergovernmental Authority on Development

IGAD's Conflict Early Warning and Response Mechanism (CEWARN), established in 2002, carries out some of the most hands-on preventive diplomacy of all international, regional, and sub-regional organizations. CEWARN's mandate is to: receive and share information concerning potentially violent conflicts as well as their outbreak and escalation in the IGAD region, undertake and share analyses of that information, develop case scenarios and formulate options for response, share and communicate information analyses and response options, and carry out studies on specific types and areas of conflict in the region.

At the heart of CEWARN is data collection and analysis, and its timely dissemination to the right people and institutions. The network of actors steered by a secretariat based in Addis Ababa was from the beginning designed to join government and civil society. It also joins regional, national and local dimensions in data collection, analysis, and decision-making.[15]

Since its establishment, CEWARN has gained valuable experience and credibility with officials and peace workers for supporting local institutions and expanding their capabilities for conflict prevention.[16] CEWARN's operations have been credited with significant reduction of violent conflict, particularly along the Kenya-Uganda and Ethiopia-Kenya-Somalia borders. It has built up a valuable body of data and knowledge on violent conflicts along IGAD member state borders and the ability to implement development projects on the ground that entrench peace by reducing the incentive for violent conflict.

Conflicts over scarce land, water, and pasture resources are prevalent in the IGAD region, where pastoralism is predominant, and they often lead to deadly violence. CEWARN opted from the beginning for regional, cross-border cooperation to tackle the root of the problem. An example of the operation of CEWARN is provided by Tigist Hailu in an article in *Rural 21: The International Journal of Rural Development*. One early evening in 2012 the CEWARN director received a message from the coordinator of

54 *Africa*

CEWARN's national early warning and response structure in Kenya, relaying a report received from field reporters on the killing of 22 Kenyan pastoralists and the theft of their cattle. The cattle had allegedly then been driven across the border into Ethiopia by armed attackers who were believed to be from a neighboring community in the country.

As the evening wore on, details of the attack were transmitted among field reporters, the national coordinators of Ethiopia and Kenya, and the CEWARN director. In less than two hours, CEWARN had briefed senior officials in both countries, leading, over the next four days, "until the perpetrators have been arrested, their weapons seized and the stolen livestock recovered."[17] Thereafter, there was a handover ceremony, carried out with the help of local officials that blended the legal state approach with the local practices of reconciliation. At the end, the relationship between the countries was strengthened by their ability to agree on a version of what had happened in an area where communication was poor, while the violence was prevented from escalating to claim even more lives and property.

CEWARN expanded its focus in 2012 following the launch of the CEWARN Strategic Framework 2012–2019. The new strategy brought in a significant expansion of its thematic focus, that is, on the types, causes, and drivers of violent conflicts beyond pastoral conflicts. Before working out the new strategy CEWARN engaged in extensive local consultations with up to 5,000 citizens and local officials, followed by consultations with national officials and NGOs in each member state. The new strategy identified 60 high priority typology themes, with detailed specification of potential problems in each IGAD member state.

The new CEWARN strategy framework recognizes that the risks and structures of violent conflict in the region are increasingly complex and interwoven. It is mindful of the need to address rapid urbanization and the conflict implications of the networks and proximities of cities, climate extremes, and the growing nexus between resource competition and violent conflict. Governance structures on the national, regional, and international levels affect the pace of sociopolitical change and evolution. A large youth population is difficult to absorb into the formal economy, and growing populations and economic development have increased the demand for natural resources and contributed to environmental degradation. The sociocultural values that inform cooperation, competition, and conflict are increasingly divorced from long-standing traditions and are driven by ideals, appetites, and worldviews from distant lands. And historical inequality among regions or center-periphery conflicts, the rapid evolution of communications and weapons technology and its democratization also need to be addressed.

Africa 55

The Southern African Development Community

Like the AU, ECOWAS, and IGAD, the Southern African Development Community has an active program of conflict prevention and preventive diplomacy that has been put to use in protracted conflicts such as those in the Democratic Republic of the Congo (DRC) and Zimbabwe—both SADC members. Since the 1990s the organization has supported mediation and preventive diplomacy efforts in the former country, being at the forefront of efforts to advance dialogue and negotiations to end the state's conflicts. For example, the 1999 Lusaka Peace Agreement and the 2002 Inter-Congolese Dialogue were facilitated by SADC leaders. In 2013, the Regional Pact on Peace and Security, and the Peace, Security and Cooperation Framework for the DRC, signed by 11 countries, sought to build stability by addressing the root causes of the conflict and fostering trust between neighbors. Efforts that have "somewhat led to the reduction of some direct forms of violence and the cessation of hostilities."[18]

SADC preventive diplomacy, with South Africa in the lead, also helped bring about the 2008 Global Political Agreement, which led to the formation of an inclusive government in Zimbabwe. After a lengthy examination of the conflict and the efforts of SADC and South Africa, Allison Marie Coady concluded that "the South Africa-led process of mediation between the disputing political parties of Zimbabwe is a valid example of preventive diplomacy." Yet, she considered that the limitations of Track One diplomacy required supplementary preventive diplomacy contributions of other actors through multi-track diplomacy.[19]

Conclusion

Perhaps more than any other part of the world, Africa has experienced conflicts due to climate change and expanding deserts. It cooperates in international efforts to turn global warming around, and the African Union is making its own contributions, such as it can.

Unfortunately, Africa continues to be wracked by conflicts the causes of which are manifold. Historical legacy plays a part inasmuch as the colonial boundaries inherited by today's African states often divide kindred ethnic communities arbitrarily between two or more states. African states are still working on issues of national cohesion due to such historical factors: the traumas of conquest and exploitation, the arbitrary separation of communities, the convulsions of the struggles for independence, the tragedy of post-colonial dictatorships, the continuing legacy of underdevelopment and inequality, and now the phenomenon of expanding deserts and the resulting crises and conflicts.

56 *Africa*

African organizations such as the AU, ECOWAS, SADC, and IGAD have undoubtedly labored valiantly to help stabilize the continent, to turn around conflicts, to provide peacemakers and peacekeepers, and to operative institutions and processes of conflict prevention and preventive diplomacy. What these organizations are having to face more and more is the impact of external powers which have divergent interests in many situations. Some external powers support terrorist movements that wreak havoc on the continent. Others are engaged in a new great game of global rivalry and seek to establish footholds, including bases, in strategic parts of Africa.

In the crisis that unfolded in Sudan after the overthrow of the former dictator Omar al-Bashir, the divergent interests of these powers impacted on AU diplomatic efforts to mediate. Nevertheless, the AU persisted and was able to help negotiate a peace agreement. Valiant efforts have been made in Africa to deploy peacekeeping forces to help contain or stabilize conflicts. However, the AU is not resource rich, and depends on the support of partners for peacekeeping efforts. With this help, African peacekeeping forces play an important role in containing conflicts and preventing their expansion. IGAD has also deployed innovative preventive diplomacy as it seeks to prevent border clashes between ethnic groups from escalating into war between their respective states. This is preventive diplomacy in the context of climate change.

As discussed in the chapter, the AU Panel of the Wise has initiated imaginative preventive diplomacy, interceding in sensitive situations to help prevent them from spilling over into conflict. Similar efforts have been seen by SADC in trying to help manage the transition in Zimbabwe from former president Robert Mugabe to a democratically-elected successor. The chapter also highlighted the AU's innovation in highlighting the role of female ambassadors for peace and seeking to get women to play a dynamic role in preventive diplomacy.

While violations of human rights continue to be numerous on the continent as, indeed, in other parts of the world, a normative architecture of protection and prevention has been developed over time by the African Commission on Human and Peoples' Rights. In the long term, this can be important in helping to prevent conflict, but it remains to be seen whether the backlash against human rights led by major powers will vitiate the efforts of bodies such as the commission.

When it comes to the implementation of SDG 16 on peace, justice, and equitable institutions, we have seen that while it has nominal support from the African Union, the organization has not so far mobilized to make an African contribution in support of its implementation.

The chapter concludes by making the firm submission that the prevention of conflicts, and preventive diplomacy in Africa, will never quite succeed

Africa 57

unless there is improvement in respect for, and protection of, human rights. The key to prevention lies in the faithful implementation of international and African norms on human rights. The African Union would therefore be wise to consider how it can strengthen the African Commission on Human and Peoples' Rights. Unfortunately, AU states have recently sought to minimize the independence of the commission. The African Union would be well advised to consider a recommendation made some years ago in Arusha that it should establish an institution similar to the OSCE high commissioner on national minorities. In short, while there is much that is admirable about African preventive diplomacy, formidable challenges persist on the continent.

Notes

1 Jeffrey D. Sachs, *The Age of Sustainable Development* (New York: Columbia University Press, 2015), 107, 112.
2 See African Union, "Environment, Climate Change, Water, Land and Natural Resources." Availableathttps://au.int/en/directorates/environment-climate-change-water-land-and-natural-resources.
3 See, Florian Krampe and Vane Moraa Aminga, "The Need for an African Union Special Envoy for Climate Change and Security," *Reliefweb*, February 7, 2019. Available at, https://reliefweb.int/report/world/need-african-union-special-envoy-climate-change-and-security.
4 This account of the efforts of the AU is based on interviews conducted, and documents obtained, at AU Headquarters in Addis Ababa in June 2019. The author is grateful to all those who helped him in his research. The AU Defense and Security Division, "Annual Newsletter 2018" was informative and the source of some of the information used here.
5 AU, "Protocol to the African Charter on Human and Peoples' Rights on the Establishment of an African Court on Human and Peoples' Rights," 1998, Article 3(f).
6 Ibid., Article 4(j).
7 Ted Robert Gurr, ed., *Minorities at Risk: A Global View of Ethnopolitical Conflicts* (Washington, DC: US Institute for Peace, 1993), 315.
8 African Commission on Human and Peoples' Rights, *Media Rights Agenda and Constitutional Rights Project v. Nigeria*, Communication No. 105793, 128/94 and 152/96, Activity Report 1998–1999, Annex V, October 31, 1998. Available at , www.worldcourts.com/achpr/eng/decisions/1998.10.31_Media_Rights_Agenda_v_Nigeria.htm. See also Malcolm Evans and Rachel Murray, *The African Charter on Human and Peoples' Rights: The System in Practice 1986–2000* (Cambridge University Press, 2008), 7. See generally, Virginia Leary, Constance Thomas, Martin Oelz, and Xavier Beaudonnet, "The Use of International Labour Law in Domestic Courts: Theory, Jurisprudence and Practical Implications," in *Les normes internationales du travail: un patrimoine pour l'avenir* (Geneva: International Labour Organization, 2004), 249–286.
9 Cited from the original decision in the possession of the author.

58 *Africa*

10 African Commission on Human and Peoples' Rights, *Constitutional Rights Project v. Nigeria*, 1996. Cited from the original decision in the possession of the author.

11 See, International IDEA and the Community of Democracy, Inter-Regional Dialogue on Democracy (IRDD), "The Role of Global and Regional Organizations in the Advancement of Sustainable Development Goal 16," Address by the Inter-Parliamentary Union (IPU) Secretary General, Martin Chungong, Geneva, March 13, 2018. Available at www.ipu.org/documents/2018-03/inter-regional-dialogue-democracy-irdd-role-global-and-regional-organizations-in-advancement-sustainable-development-goal-16.

12 ECOWAS, "Plans of Action for the 15 Components of the ECOWAS Conflict Prevention Framework," undated, circa 2017.

13 Samuel M. Makinda, F. Wafula Okumu, and David Mickler, *The African Union: Addressing the Challenges of Peace, Security and Governance*, 2nd ed. (London: Routledge, 2016), 108–112.

14 Ibid.

15 See on this, Tigist Hailu, "Data-Based Conflict Early Warning: A Vital Instrument in Peacebuilding," *New Routes* no. 4, 2012, 24–26.

16 This account of the activities of CEWARN is based on interviews conducted and information obtained at IGAD's headquarters in Addis Ababa in June 2019. I am particularly grateful to Tigist Hailu for her insights and assistance.

17 Tigist Hailu, "Anticipate and Prevent Violent Conflicts," *Rural 21*, no. 1, 2012, 18.

18 Martha Mutisi, "SADC Interventions in the Democratic Republic of the Congo," *ACCORD*, October 19, 2016. Available at www.accord.org.za/conflict-trends/sadc-interventions-democratic-republic-congo/.

19 Allison Marie Coady, "Examining the Role of Preventive Diplomacy in South Africa's Foreign Policy towards Zimbabwe, 2000–2009," Master's thesis, Department of Political Sciences, University of Pretoria, South Africa, December 2012, 180.

3 Asia
ASEAN and other sub-regional institutions and proposals

- ASEAN
- Other institutions and proposals
- Conclusion

Asia has no intergovernmental organizations that span the entire continent. Of its various sub-regional organizations, the most prominent is the Association of Southeast Asian Nations, whose 10 member states conduct diplomatic relations and coordinate activity in a broad range of policy areas. In contrast, institutions and mechanisms in other regions of Asia tend to be extremely weak. Consequently, this chapter will primarily focus on discussing ASEAN initiatives. It will then make a more cursory examination of organizations elsewhere in Asia: the Arab League's Peace and Security Council, the Asia Cooperation Dialogue, and the Shanghai Cooperation Organization. Finally, the chapter analyzes an Iranian proposal for a regional dialogue forum in the Persian Gulf, and proposals contained in a 2017 report on the "Institutional Building Blocks of Long-Term Regional Security."

ASEAN

ASEAN operates in the backyard of powerful China, and under the outreach of the United States, both of which increasingly constrain the organization's room for action. Its preventive diplomacy seems to have stalled and to be riding on past efforts, even if it has had pronouncements on all five themes we are exploring in this book—climate change, weapons of mass destruction, conflicts, sustainable development, and human rights. Its work on human rights, though possessing a few preventive dimensions, is somewhat lacking in relation to gross violations. Each of the themes is examined in turn below.

60 *Asia*

Climate change

ASEAN considers that Southeast Asia is one of the regions most at risk from climate change, with forecasted rankings showing that six of the 20 countries most vulnerable worldwide are situated here: Indonesia, Thailand, Myanmar, Malaysia, Vietnam, and the Philippines. Specific multi-hazard hotspots include many of the populated Indonesian islands, the Chao Phraya Delta in Thailand, the Ayeyarwady (Irrawaddy) Delta in Myanmar, the Mekong Delta in Cambodia and Vietnam, the eastern coastline of Vietnam up to the Red River Delta, and Manila and other zones across the Philippines.[1] Southeast Asia is highly vulnerable to climate change because a large proportion of the population and economic activity are concentrated along coastlines, while the region is also heavily reliant on agriculture and there is a high dependence on natural resources and forestry.

An ASEAN Working Group on Climate Change (AWGCC) was established in 2009 as a consultative and collaborative effort to enhance regional cooperation and action to address the adverse impacts of climate change on socio-economic development in member states, including through cooperation and information sharing with other stakeholders—private sector, local community, regional, and international partners.

The AWGCC is also mandated to formulate the region's interests, concerns, and priorities in an ASEAN Joint Statement on Climate Change articulated at annual sessions of the United Nations Framework Convention on Climate Change Conference of the Parties (UNFCC COP). The AWGCC also serves as a consultative forum to promote coordination and collaboration amongst ASEAN bodies dealing with sectors impacted by climate change, such as energy, forestry, agriculture, transportation, science and technology, and disaster management, in order to enhance the coordination and integration of efforts to address climate change.

Collectively, member states have been responding to the issue by focusing on the implementation of actions in the ASEAN Socio-Cultural Community (ASCC) Blueprint 2025. In this endeavor, AWGCC is guided by an Action Plan, which comprises priority actions until 2025.

Weapons of mass destruction

The ASEAN Charter of 2007 prohibits nuclear, chemical, and biological weapons in its member states, re-endorsing an earlier treaty adopted to keep Southeast Asia free of nuclear weapons, all other weapons of mass destruction, and interference by external powers. Already in 1971, the original five members of ASEAN had agreed on a declaration on an ASEAN

Asia 61

Zone of Peace, Freedom, and Neutrality (ZOPFAN). Its first pillar was the establishment of the Southeast Asian Nuclear-Weapon-Free-Zone (SEANWFZ) Treaty (also known as the Bangkok Treaty), signed by the heads of state and government of all ten ASEAN states in Bangkok on December 15, 1995.

Under the Bangkok Treaty, state parties agree to a wide range of restrictions, including not to develop, manufacture, or otherwise acquire, possess, or have control over nuclear weapons; not to station, test, or use them anywhere inside or outside the treaty zone; not to dump radioactive waste and other radioactive matter at sea anywhere within the zone, and to prevent dumping by others in their territorial seas.

The treaty zone covers the territories, continental shelves, and exclusive economic zones of the state parties. Verification is carried out through reports by members and exchange of information, and the application of International Atomic Energy Agency (IAEA) safeguards. The treaty provides for a Commission for the Southeast Asia Nuclear-Weapon-Free Zone to oversee its implementation and ensure compliance. It also gives each state party the right to ask another for clarification or a fact-finding mission to resolve an ambiguous situation or one which may give rise to doubts about compliance. The commission can decide on measures it deems appropriate to cope with a party that is out of compliance, including the submission of the matter to the IAEA and, where the situation might endanger international peace and security, the Security Council and the General Assembly of the UN.[2]

Conflicts and violence

Consensual preventive diplomacy has been at the heart of ASEAN's mission since its establishment in 1967. This has entailed dialogue and consultations among state leaders as well as deliberations within the ASEAN Regional Forum (ARF), which consists of representatives of the major powers across the globe in addition to the organization's member states. ASEAN's preventive diplomacy has registered significant achievements in the past, such as with its efforts to contain and manage the conflict in Cambodia.

ASEAN's preventive diplomacy relies on diplomatic and peaceful methods such as negotiation, enquiry, mediation, and conciliation; it is non-coercive. And it is conducted in accordance with universally recognized principles of international law and inter-state relations embodied, inter alia, in the UN Charter and the Five Principles of Peaceful Co-Existence (the Panchsheel Treaty).[3]

The ASEAN Charter provides significant opportunities for the exercise of preventive diplomacy. These include the roles of: permanent representatives

62 *Asia*

of ASEAN members accredited to the organization; the ASEAN secretary-general; strategic institutes within ASEAN countries; and civil society. The charter spells out the ground rules for the conduct of ASEAN preventive diplomacy. These start with the purposes of ASEAN, stated in Article 1 to include: maintaining and enhancing peace, security and stability, and further strengthening peace-oriented values in the region; the alleviation of poverty and narrowing the development gap within ASEAN through mutual assistance and cooperation; strengthening democracy, and enhancing good governance and the rule of law; promoting and protecting human rights and fundamental freedoms; responding to all forms of threats, trans-national crimes, and trans-boundary challenges; promoting sustainable development and preserving cultural heritage; and enhancing the well-being and livelihood of the peoples of ASEAN by providing them with equitable access to opportunities for human development, social welfare, and justice.

The charter established an ASEAN Coordinating Council comprising members' foreign ministers, who meet at least twice a year. It also provides for ASEAN Community Councils which comprise the Political-Security Community Council, Economic Community Council, and Socio-Cultural Community Council. Each ASEAN member state is required to appoint a permanent representative with the rank of ambassador based in Jakarta, collectively constituting a committee; and a secretariat to serve as the national focal point and contribute to ASEAN community building. The charter also requires all members to endeavor to peacefully resolve all disputes through dialogue and negotiation. Parties to a dispute may request the ASEAN secretary-general or chairman, acting in an *ex-officio* capacity, to provide good offices, conciliation, or mediation.

The secretary-general, assisted by the secretariat or any other designated ASEAN body, is given a mandate to monitor the compliance with the findings, recommendations, or decisions resulting from an ASEAN dispute settlement mechanism, and submit a report to the ASEAN summit. Any member affected by non-compliance may refer the matter to the summit for a decision.[4]

Such provisions give scope for meaningful preventive diplomacy. Unfortunately, in recent years they have existed more on paper than in practice. Partly responsible is that many of the disputes and conflicts in the region are internal, involving contesting ethnic groups or minorities. ASEAN officials have not been ready to play a preventive or peacemaking role in relation to such conflicts. The secretary-general has been rather passive and the secretariat itself has sparse resources. Overall, ASEAN has been unwilling to face up to serious violations of human rights within its midst, and the ASEAN Intergovernmental Commission on Human Rights (AICHR) has so far been rather mild in its approaches.

Asia 63

Human rights

The Intergovernmental Commission on Human Rights has come in for much criticism as a body of governmental representatives that has so far declined to deal with allegations of gross violations of human rights. Still, the case can be made that, in the circumstances of ASEAN politics, with its emphasis on consensual approaches to dealing with problems, AICHR does make a modest contribution to prevention. This takes the form of efforts to sensitize member governments and the wider ASEAN public on threats and challenges and to help develop policy frameworks for prevention and protection over time.

In 2015 AICHR held workshops in Myanmar and the Philippines on the implementation of human rights obligations relating to the environment and climate change. Some of the topics discussed included the gap between legislation and implementation, the plight of marginalized and vulnerable groups, and the necessity to have a fuller grasp of the problems so as to contribute to a possible regional framework. An earlier workshop on the topic had been held in Myanmar in 2014. Participants at the workshops emphasized that there was a clear connection between human rights and environmental sustainability/climate change and urged the adoption of a human rights base to environmental policymaking.

An AICHR Dialogue was held in Indonesia in 2013 with the topic of "Building a Torture-Free ASEAN Community." One of its recurring concerns was the disparity of human rights standards within ASEAN, as not all members had ratified the UN Convention against Torture. AICHR has also highlighted the importance of prevention strategies to combat people trafficking, and to enhance access to information and community-based protection. A regional workshop on the topic was held in Vietnam in 2019; earlier workshops on the same subject were held in the country in 2015 and 2016.

AICHR has also sought to share experience among ASEAN governments on international human rights law. This was the topic of a judicial colloquium held in Malaysia in 2017. An earlier workshop, held in Laos in 2014, explored the sharing of national experiences on human rights implementation. The same year, workshops also focused on sharing experiences on the Universal Periodic Review, and the reporting obligations of member states under human rights treaties.

Other relevant AICHR initiatives include women's economic empowerment, in an AICHR Forum in Singapore in 2018, and a thematic study on migration, with a consultation on this in 2013. It has also undertaken a study on the right to peace and has held regional workshops on the topic with the purpose of promoting a culture of peace.

64 *Asia*

AICHR is currently in the first decade of its existence and has so far not had much of a record of achievement in actually protecting human rights. However, from the activities cited above, it would be fair to say that it is endeavoring to contribute to a human rights ethic within the region which will hopefully encourage the promotion and protection of human rights, and the prevention of violations in the long term. The right to peace, the prevention of torture, the prevention of trafficking in human beings, the empowerment of women, a regulatory framework for migration, and the implementation of international human rights law are all topics that, over time, may contribute to a culture of prevention of gross violations and protection of human rights in the region.

SDG 16

ASEAN's Vision 2025 emphasizes strengthening democracy, good governance, and the rule of law, the promotion and protection of human rights and fundamental freedoms, and combating corruption to raise the standard of living within the region—all elements of SDG 16. ASEAN has started to incorporate the relevant SDG anti-corruption and good governance targets as key indicators in constructing the ASEAN Integrity Dialogue, the mechanism to promote anti-corruption proposed in the ASEAN 2016–2025 work plan. This includes targets related to tackling corruption and bribery, stopping illegal financial flows both within and outside of the region, the enactment and implementation of a right to information laws realizing people's right to search for, receive, and impart information and building strong institutions, including a network of strong anti-corruption commissions in the region embracing the 2012 Jakarta Statement on Principles for Anti-Corruption Agencies (the Jakarta principles).[5]

The UN 2030 Agenda for Sustainable Development specified that member states should "conduct regular and inclusive reviews of progress at the national and sub-national levels, which are country-led and country-driven." When the UN High Level Political Forum (HLPF) holds its yearly meetings under the auspices of ECOSOC it should carry out regular reviews that are voluntary and state-led, involving ministerial and other relevant high-level participants, and involving developed and developing countries. The reviews are to "provide a platform for partnerships, including through the participation of major groups and other relevant stakeholders."

Two ASEAN countries submitted reports for the 2019 HLPF review: Indonesia and the Philippines. The Indonesian report dealt with empowering people and ensuring inclusiveness and equality; inclusive and consistent economic growth; achieving near-universal education; managing disaster;

Asia 65

realizing access to justice and inclusive institutions; innovative development financing; broad, inclusive national process and strategic global partnership; overcoming challenges; and the way forward. The section on access to justice and inclusive institutions referred to an improvement in Indonesia's democracy index, anti-corruption behavior index, birth registrations, and legal aid to the poor.

The Philippine report contained sections on quality education; decent work; reduction of inequality; climate action; peace, justice, and strong institutions; and ensuring the effectiveness of partnerships. On peace, justice, and strong institutions, the report stated that a major milestone had been the ratification of the Bangsamoro Organic Law, the result of cumulative initiatives, including those by the international community, to address a long-standing conflict in southern Philippines.

Other institutions and proposals

The Middle East and Asia present some of the gravest dangers to international peace and security, but, with the limited exception of ASEAN, for the most part lack institutions or arrangements for the prevention of conflicts or for preventive diplomacy. Worse still, because of great power dominance, there is little room for the exercise of preventive diplomacy in relation to potentially deadly conflicts. The UN Security Council and secretary-general choose, given the nature of things, largely to abstain from initiatives to prevent conflict, even if they do engage in specious exchanges on cooperation with the Arab League.

In the Middle East, it is an open secret that Israel possesses nuclear weapons and Iran has been trying to obtain them as well. The 2015 Joint Comprehensive Plan of Action (JCPOA) was negotiated to help delay Iran's development of nuclear weapons, but the United States, under President Trump, withdrew from the agreement and, at the time of writing, in fall 2019, its future is uncertain, to say the least. If Iran does eventually come close to obtaining nuclear weapons, there is a strong likelihood that it will come under attack from Israel and/or the United States. What is more, if Iran does come close, countries such as Saudi Arabia, an archrival of Iran in the region, will in likelihood seek to obtain them as well. During 2019 there have been tense exchanges between Western powers and Iran over the free passage of oil tankers through the Strait of Hormuz. President Trump has publicly warned Iran not to interfere with US ships.

In addition to the dangerous contexts of Israeli–Iranian and US–Iranian relations, there are at least three other scenarios of concern in the wider Asia region. There is the continuing stand-off between the Koreas, and between North Korea and the United States. In the South China Sea there

66 *Asia*

continue to be testing face-offs between China and the United States, and seasoned commentators are of the view that the odds are on a clash between these two global powers.[6]

A fifth dangerous situation involves two nuclear-armed powers, India and Pakistan, which have fought wars before over Kashmir and, at the time of writing, are again in a tense stand-off over the territory. The passions on both sides are so strong that it is difficult to envisage any institutional organization of preventive diplomacy between them, even if influential powers might be able to play a role behind the scene. Both countries are members of the Shanghai Cooperation Organization, which includes China and Russia, and one hopes that the leadership of these two countries might play a stabilizing role, even if China is openly an ally of Pakistan and Russia has had historically close relations with India.

There are various sources of strategic insecurity for the region's future. First and foremost is North Korea's nuclear weapons program. In addition to those mentioned above, others include tensions over the East China Sea, the Sino-Indian border (a long-unresolved issue), massively increasing Asian military budgets (which overall overtook those of Europe for the first time in 2015), a range of tensions between ethnic groups, and domestic insurgencies.[7]

In this book, we have sought to examine the preventive efforts, such as they are, of the organizations discussed in relation to five topics: climate change, weapons of mass destruction, conflict prevention, gross violations of human rights, and SDG 16. When it comes to the Middle East and Asia there are no comprehensive organizations to provide a context for a thorough thematic examination. This section therefore limits itself to the issue of conflict prevention and preventive diplomacy.

The existing or proposed institutional arrangements that will be discussed here include the Arab League's Peace and Security Council, which theoretically covers the Middle East; the Asian Cooperation Dialogue (ACD); the Shanghai Cooperation Organization (SCO); and the Iranian proposal for a Regional Dialogue. The discussion ends with important proposals in a recent report by the Asia Society Policy Institute to enhance arrangements for conflict prevention and preventive diplomacy in the Asia-Pacific region.

The Arab League's Peace and Security Council

Historically, the Arab League has not played much of a mediatory or preventive role. A close analyst of the absence of conflict prevention mechanisms in the Middle East has written that the Middle East is marked by various forms of state failure, civil conflict, interstate tensions, and transnational threats, and that that reality is likely to remain a defining feature of the region. More to the point,

> [t]he region is also sorely lacking, perhaps uniquely, in its collective capacity to prevent and manage conflict. A full-fledged regional security architecture that includes robust conflict prevention mechanisms has long been seen as a desirable goal. Nonetheless, discussions ... have obviously proven elusive.[8]

The Arab League was established in 1945 as the League of Arab States with a mandate to engage in conflict prevention and other kinds of peace and security activities. Article 5 of its charter gives the Council of the League a mandate to mediate in disputes that may lead to war between member states or between a member and another state. However, this mandate has hardly been used and although limited efforts have been made to build up the institutional framework of the Arab League's peace and security activities, these efforts have remained "stunted."[9]

In 2006 the Arab League sought to emulate the African Union and to establish an Arab Peace and Security Council to prevent, manage, and resolve regional conflicts. This was, in fact, formally established in 2008 but remains advisory in function, with its recommendations subject to approval by the Arab League Council. Unfortunately, the league opted against other innovations, such as the proposed establishment of a data bank, early warning system, and a "panel of the wise"—a select group of experienced leaders with the credentials to act as conflict mediators. In sum, "the reforms are mostly notional, but the resulting institutional steps nonetheless provide an existing basis and framework upon which reforms could be based if political will crystallizes in the future."[10]

The Asia Cooperation Dialogue

The ACD was established in 2002 in Cha-Am, Thailand. It currently has 31 member states, from across Asia, including global and regional powers such as Russia, China, Japan, and India, as well as smaller states such as Bahrain, Bangladesh, Kyrgyzstan, Malaysia, the Philippines, and Singapore.

The ACD seeks to cooperate in 19 areas, including energy, information and communications technology, and transport. Project selection and implementation proceed on a voluntary basis and need not require a consensus from all members. Its policy orientations are expressed in the ACD Vision for Asian Cooperation 2030, the ACD Blueprint for 2017–2021, and ACD Summit Declarations. While there is no explicit conflict prevention

68 *Asia*

mandate in its terms of reference, the very fact that the foreign ministers of ACD countries meet regularly could provide opportunities for discreet exchanges with a view to calming trouble-spots.

The Shanghai Cooperation Organization

The SCO was established in 2001 for the purpose of political, military, and economic cooperation, and currently consists of eight states: India, Kazakhstan, China, Kyrgyzstan, Pakistan, Russia, Tajikistan, and Uzbekistan. A focus of the organization is fighting terrorism, separatism, and extremism.

Information security has been of particular concern. During a meeting of the SCO national security council secretaries on May 21–22, 1999 in Beijing it was stressed that information and communications technology, including the Internet, were being actively used to promote terrorism, separatism and extremism, to recruit militants, to expand terrorist activities, and to interfere in the domestic affairs of other states as well as to commit other criminal acts.[11] At a meeting in Kyrgyzstan in June, SCO leaders signed a joint declaration calling for greater cooperation among member states and reaffirming their intent to ensure security for their region. The talks focused on expanding cooperation on security, fighting terrorism and drug trafficking, economic development, industry, and humanitarian cooperation.[12] See Box 3.1 below for deliberations within the UN Security Council in September 2019 on efforts by the SCO and other Asian and European organizations in combating terrorism.

Box 3.1 Cooperation between the UN and Asian and European multilateral organizations on combating terrorism

Deliberations in the UN Security Council, September 25, 2019

Secretary-General Antonio Guterres welcomed the move to increase cooperation between the UN and the Collective Security Treaty Organization (CSTO), the Commonwealth of Independent States (CIS), and the Shanghai Cooperation Organization (SCO) on Wednesday [September 25, 2019]. His message came at the start of a ministerial-level debate in the Security Council on the role of the three bodies ...

Mr Guterres outlined the "unprecedented threat" posed by intolerance, violent extremism and terrorism, including cyber-terrorism which, he said, is constantly evolving and affects every country. The UN, he continued, has a comprehensive framework for action, provided by the Organization's Global Counter-Terrorism Strategy ...

Asia 69

Address root causes, promote gender equality, respect human rights

Whilst security measures to pursue and dismantle terrorist groups are "vital," they must be complemented by efforts to identify and address root causes, counselled the Secretary-General, such as fear and hopelessness, while always respecting human rights.

"We must reinforce the social compact, including the provision of basic services and opportunities, particularly for young people. Most recruits to terrorist groups are between 17 and 27 years old. We need to provide paths that offer a sense of hope and purpose to our young men and women, including education, training and jobs."

The frequent subjugation of women and girls, which is a "foundational" purpose of many extremist and terrorist groups, was raised by Mr Guterres, who said that gender equality and engaging women and girls must be central to efforts to prevent and counter terrorism: "Terrorist groups share an agenda that is authoritarian, intolerant and frequently misogynistic. Our efforts to counter terrorist ideology must be founded on respect for the dignity and human rights of all."

Turning to the specific role of the three organizations at the centre of Wednesday's debate, Mr Guterres noted that countries need to cooperate in order to meet cross-border challenges such as the return and relocation of foreign terrorist fighters, and include private sector and civil society partners in these efforts.

The UN chief stressed that the UN is strengthening its institutional links with each of them, establishing frameworks for joint activities, and collaboration on capacity-building assistance. He singled out the UN Joint Plan of Action for the Implementation of the Global Counter-Terrorism Strategy in Central Asia ... as showing what can be achieved with collective action, leadership and political will.

Sergei Lavrov, Russian Minister for Foreign Affairs, [the President of the Security Council for the month of September], said that more needs to be done to work together with regional and sub-regional organizations, such as the three bodies under discussion at the debate (CSTO, CIS, and SCO).

These organizations, he said, have a "rich experience of fighting terrorism and contribute to stability in the Eurasian continent. Their activity is a gauge of security of their Member States, and the effective counter-terrorism efforts they undertake help noticeably to stabilize the situation in Central Asia."

Mr Lavrov expressed concern at ongoing recruitment by various terror groups in the region, and noted that the CSTO is working to close recruitment channels and illegal migration, as well as paying close attention to the role of the internet in spreading extremist ideologies. He welcomed the commitment from all three organizations to further broadening cooperation in the area of combating terrorism within the UN, in order to maintain regional and international peace and security.

Source: UN News, "Security Council Debates Closer Links between Multilateral Organizations in Europe and Asia," September 25, 2019

70 *Asia*

An Iranian proposal for a regional dialogue forum in the Persian Gulf

On a number of occasions, Foreign Minister Mohammad Javad Zarif of Iran has shared his view that there is a "dialogue deficiency" in the Persian Gulf which could be resolved by the establishment of a "regional dialogue forum" in the region. Addressing the sixteenth meeting of the ACD in Doha on May 1, 2019, he stated that:

> Every player in our region should understand that we are neighbors forever, and that the only way to secure peace and prosperity is through the recognition of a common destiny. And an acceptance that inclusive multilateral dialogue is the only way out of the current multidimensional crises facing us all.[13]

However, the Iranian government has not so far spelled out a blueprint for the proposed forum and it is not clear whether there are active conversations with Gulf states on the matter. In any event, relations between Iran and Saudi Arabia are so conflicted at the present time, with the United States taking a trenchant position in favor of Saudi Arabia and against Iran, that it is difficult to see this idea taking off at the present time. Nevertheless, intrinsically, the idea has merit and could, in the long term, serve as a forum to defuse tensions and promote cooperation.

2017 report on the "Institutional Building Blocks of Long-Term Regional Security"

The report, whose full name is "Preserving the Long Peace in Asia: The Institutional Building Blocks of Long-Term Regional Security," was authored by a group including a former prime minister of Australia (as chair); former national security advisers of the United States and India; former foreign ministers of Japan, Russia, and, South Korea; and a high-level Chinese academic, the director of the Institute of American Studies at the Chinese Academy of Social Sciences.

It argues that strategic disagreements are often better managed within the framework of regional institutions anchored in commonly accepted norms and that one can use effective regional institutions to take down the regional temperature over time. The report cautions about the growing strategic competition between major players in Asia. As China rises and other Asia-Pacific nations adapt to evolving power dynamics in the region, leading powers are experiencing newfound friction points in their bilateral relations. Furthermore, growing strategic competition between the United

Asia 71

States and China has implications for the wider security architecture as the deepening geopolitical gaps between the two countries create schisms in the region. One of the greatest threats in the rapidly militarizing region is the risk of inadvertent crisis and/or military escalation.

To provide a stronger central core for Asia's security architecture, the report recommends that ASEAN-based institutions remain the centerpiece. A central role is foreseen for the ASEAN permanent representatives based in its Jakarta headquarters. The ASEAN Charter could also be strengthened to allow for more flexible applications of consensus, and for the establishment of a nongovernmental Eminent Persons Group to propose concrete regional confidence-building measures. These could include the improvement of understanding of regional principles, such as the "Bali Principles," the 2011 Declaration of the East Asia Summit on the Principles for Mutually Beneficial Relations.

Most importantly, the report focused on the role of the East Asia Summit (EAS), which consists of the United States, Russia, Japan, South Korea, India, Australia, New Zealand, and the 10 members of ASEAN. It argued that the EAS should be another central node of a broader regional network, with all non-ASEAN members designating an individual as their permanent representative to ASEAN. This could also be used as a starting point for an informal crisis management mechanism. The ASEAN secretariat could provide institutional support for the EAS in the short term, pending the establishment of a floating EAS secretariat.

States should commit to further strengthening and enhancing the role of the EAS as a leader-level forum. EAS members could take initial steps to provide it with a more operational role, enabling it to act meaningfully in preventive diplomacy, establishing crisis management protocols, and identifying confidence-building mechanisms. Of particular interest for this book, the report recommends that EAS members establish crisis prevention and dispute resolution mechanisms: "Member States could create real operational capabilities for the EAS by considering the establishment of formal crisis prevention and risk reduction mechanisms, such as a multinational Risk Reduction Centre."

Conclusion

ASEAN has a respectable history of consensual preventive diplomacy and has made notable contributions in situations such as the Cambodian conflict. ASEAN performs an important role through its Regional Forum, which assembles member states as well as major external powers to help contain situations of concern. ASEAN has sought, so far not successfully, to work out with China a set of principles to guide the conduct of future

72   Asia

relations among Asian powers. Such a statement of principles could be crucial in helping to manage future relations between a powerful, assertive China and its neighbors in the region.

The Asia Society Policy Institute report highlighted the importance of concluding a statement of principles in the near future.[14] The commission suggested, perhaps not wisely, that ASEAN should consider moving away somewhat from the principle of consensus in taking decisions to one of deciding by majority.

The organization has also sought to make its region a "nuclear-free zone," an important contribution to dealing with the threat from weapons of mass destruction. Unfortunately, the wider Asian region is a theater of mounting great power rivalries, and it is to be hoped that any clash between China and the United States, for example, will not involve the use of WMDs.

The situation of minorities and indigenous populations in Asia give cause for serious concern. ASEAN might lead the way in preventive diplomacy to manage such situations with justice. Gross violations of human rights continue to be rampant in many parts of Asia, while the ASEAN Intergovernmental Commission on Human Rights has a rather weak mandate and composition, consisting not of independent experts but of representatives of governments. The commission has initiated some useful deliberations on structural issues affecting the realization of human rights and, to that extent, might be considered to have made a modest contribution to the prevention of gross violations of human rights. Lastly, ASEAN's contribution to the implementation of SDG 16 has so far not been substantial and one can only hope that this will change speedily.

Overall, it would probably be fair to say that although ASEAN has a vaunted reputation for preventive diplomacy, it is, for the most part, relying on past laurels and hardly making a worthwhile contribution at the present. The Asia Society Policy Institute commission saw potential in the role of the group of ASEAN permanent representatives based in Jakarta and also in a future role for the ASEAN secretary-general. They recognized, however, that member states would need to provide the secretariat with more resources to allow it to develop a more vibrant role in contemporary preventive diplomacy.

In regard to other organizations and proposals, the central conclusion is that while there are dangerous conflicts in the Middle East and the wider Asian region at the present time, there is great need for the enhancement of institutions dedicated to conflict prevention and preventive diplomacy. In addition to the deep-seated religious dimensions of some of the key conflicts in the Middle East, the United States is a leading partisan in several of the disputes and conflicts and it is difficult to envisage initiatives for

Asia 73

preventive diplomacy in these circumstances. China and Russia are also parties or partisans in some of these conflicts, which makes the situation overall particularly worrisome.

Great power divergences in the UN Security Council largely preclude a role for that body, and the UN secretary-general, trying to navigate his organization in the treacherous waters of great power conflicts, has so far not been able to play a role, except possibly appealing to the parties behind the scenes. This is a sobering conclusion. The recommendations of the report by the Asia Society Policy Institute for the further development of institutions and processes of conflict prevention and preventive diplomacy make much sense and are deserving of urgent attention.

Notes

1 See *ASEAN Cooperation on Climate Change*. Available at https://environment. asean.org/awgcc.
2 See NTI, Southeast Asian Nuclear-Weapon-Free-Zone (SEANWFZ) Treaty (Bangkok Treaty). Available at www.nti.org/learn/treaties-and-regimes/ southeast-asian-nuclear-weapon-free-zone-seanwfz-treaty-bangkok-treaty.
3 ASEAN Regional Forum, "Concept and Principles of Preventive Diplomacy," adopted at the eighth ASEAN Regional Forum, July 25, 2001, reproduced in Institute of Defence and Strategic Studies, *A New Agenda for the ASEAN Regional Forum*, monograph no. 4 (Singapore: Institute of Defence and Strategic Studies, 2002), 88–93.
4 See ibid., Articles 1, 8, 9, 13, 14, 22, 23, and 27.
5 See International IDEA and Community of Democracies, Inter-Regional Dialogue on Democracy (IRDD), "The Role of Global and Regional Organizations in the Advancement of Sustainable Development Goal 16," Address by the Inter-Parliamentary Union (IPU) Secretary General, Martin Chungong, Geneva, March 13, 2018. Available at www.ipu.org/documents/2018-03/inter-regional-dialogue-democracy-irdd-role-global-and-regional-organizations-in-advancement-sustainable-development-goal-16.
6 See, for example, Oystein Tunsjo, *The Return of Bi-Polarity in World Politics: China, the United States, and Geostructural Realism* (New York: Columbia University Press, 2019). Chapter 6, "US-China Relations and the Risk of War," is particularly interesting. The author considers that while all-out war involving weapons of mass destruction is unlikely because of the costs to both countries, war between them in the South China Seas is likely.
7 Independent Commission on Regional Security Architecture, "Preserving the Long Peace in Asia: The Institutional Building Blocks of Long-Term Regional Security," Asia Society Policy Institute, New York, September 2017, 10. Available at https://asiasociety.org/policy-institute/preserving-long-peace-asia.
8 Michael Wahid Hanna, "Begin the Begin: Seeding Conflict Prevention Mechanisms in the Middle East," *The Century Foundation*, March 23, 2018. Available at https://tcf.org/content/report/begin-the-begin?agreed=1.
9 Ibid.
10 Ibid., 5.

74 *Asia*

11 See NATO Cooperative Cyber Defence Centre of Excellence (CCDCOE), Shanghai Cooperation Organisation. Available at https://ccdcoe.org/organisations/sco/.

12 See Radio Free Europe/Radio Liberty, "Shanghai Cooperation Organization Members Sign Joint Declaration," June 14, 2019. Available at www.rferl.org/a/shanghai-cooperation-organization-members-sign-joint-declaration/29999988.html.

13 *Iran Front Page*, "Iran Calls for Establishment of 'Regional Dialogue' Forum,"May1,2019.Availableathttps://ifpnews.com/Iran-calls-for-establishment-of-regional-dialogue-forum.

14 Independent Commission on Regional Security Architecture, "Preserving the Long Peace in Asia."

4 The Americas and Europe
The OAS and OSCE

- The Americas: The OAS
- Europe: The OSCE
- Conclusion

This chapter, on preventive diplomacy work by intergovernmental organizations in the Western Hemisphere and in Europe, focuses in the former case on the Organization of American States, and in the latter on the Organization for Security and Cooperation in Europe. While both organizations have established mechanisms and subsidiary bodies that deal with related issues, the OAS labors under the domination of the United States, in contrast to the somewhat more balanced intergovernmental relations within the OSCE.

The Americas: The OAS

The Organization of American States, headquartered in Washington, DC, the capital of the United States, was historically a tool of that country and continues to be under its shadow. Its room for preventive diplomacy is severely constrained by the policies of whichever US administration is in power, as we see currently in regard to the situation in Venezuela. The United States is a direct partisan in that conflict, openly asserting the Monroe doctrine, and OAS preventive diplomacy is constrained by that fact. Nevertheless, there have been occasions in the past when Latin American leaders could deploy peace diplomacy despite the direct involvement of the United States in conflicts, as occurred in the case of the Contadora process during the conflicts in Central America in the 1980s.

With all its constraints, the OAS has sought to contribute to the campaign against climate change. It has an innovative organ, the Committee on Hemispheric Security, that is mandated to undertake horizon scanning with a view to detecting potential crises or conflicts. The OAS does contribute to

76 *The Americas and Europe*

peacemaking, peacekeeping, and peacebuilding as it did recently in Haiti and has impressive human rights institutions that have developed a significant jurisprudence of prevention. Unfortunately, the main human rights body of the OAS, Inter-American Commission on Human Rights, is under attack from powerful member states. In the American region, as elsewhere, the OAS is a victim of its own governments, some powerful, some recalcitrant, many undemocratic, and many oppressive. More and more, also, external powers such as China, Russia, Iran, and Turkey are having an impact on the politics of Latin America. These issues are discussed in the chapter below, which analyzes the record of the OAS in relation to our five themes. Only conflicts and violence, and human rights have seen much activity, and so these are discussed in depth before the other topics are briefly touched on.

Conflicts and violence

While the OAS has, on paper, a good normative and institutional architecture for preventive diplomacy, they do not yield much in the way of results in practice because of the dominant influence of the United States, the impact of other powers, divisions among the membership, and economic and social problems in most member countries.[1] Nevertheless, from the point of view of a scholarly study of contemporary preventive diplomacy, there are noteworthy aspects to the OAS experience that we shall highlight.

Preventive diplomacy within the OAS is envisaged in the 1947 Inter-American Treaty of Reciprocal Assistance (Rio Treaty), the 1948 Charter of the OAS, and the 1948 Inter-American Treaty on Pacific Settlement (Pact of Bogota). The latter provides for good offices and mediation by a government or private citizen in a conflict, as agreed by the parties. It also provides for investigation and conciliation under the authority of a commission of five members established by the OAS Permanent Council. Resort to arbitration and judicial settlement is also envisaged.

Preventive diplomacy in the OAS may also be exercised through the good offices of the secretary-general as well as through member states. Classic cases of such diplomacy include the negotiated settlement of conflicts in Central America in the 1980s and 1990s at the initiative of Oscar Arias, then President of Costa Rica, supported by the secretaries-general of the OAS and United Nations.

Following the Al Qaeda attacks on the United States on 9/11, the OAS convened a special conference on security in Mexico City on October 27–28, 2003. This adopted the Declaration on Security in the Americas, in which member states recognized that their security was affected, in

The Americas and Europe 77

different ways, by traditional threats and various new threats, concerns, and challenges. Some of these include:

- Terrorism, transnational organized crime, the global drug problem, corruption, asset laundering, illicit trafficking in weapons, and the connections among them;
- Extreme poverty and social exclusion of broad sectors of the population, which also affect stability and democracy;
- Natural and man-made disasters, HIV/AIDS and other diseases, other health risks, and environmental degradation;
- Trafficking in persons;
- Attacks to cyber-security;
- The potential for damage to arise in the event of an accident or incident during the maritime transport of potentially hazardous materials; and
- the possibility of access, possession, and use of weapons of mass destruction and their means of delivery by terrorists.

OAS member states affirmed that conflict prevention and the peaceful settlement of disputes between states were essential to the stability and security of the hemisphere, and recognized the importance of dialogue and other national efforts to achieve resolution of situations of internal conflict to attain reconciliation and a just and lasting peace.

OAS member states also recommended that the organization's Permanent Council, through the Committee on Hemispheric Security, continue the process of studying and assessing the Rio Treaty and Pact of Bogota; and that:

> periodically the Committee on Hemispheric Security meet as the "Forum for Confidence and Security-Building Measures" in order to review and evaluate existing confidence and security-building measures and, if appropriate, consider new measures that will make it possible to ensure progress in this area.

In pursuit of some of these aims under the declaration, the OAS also established a Secretariat for Multidimensional Security (SMS).

The SMS's mission is to promote and coordinate cooperation among the OAS member states, and between them and the Inter-American system and other international bodies, in order to assess, prevent, confront, and respond effectively to threats to security with a view to being the leading point of reference in the hemisphere for developing cooperation and capacity building. The sphere of activity of the SMS is defined by the Declaration

78 *The Americas and Europe*

on Security in the Americas and its new concept of "hemispheric security" as being multidimensional and comprising traditional threats and new threats, concerns, and challenges. The SMS has offices that deal with "multidimensional security," drug abuse control, terrorism, public security, and transnational organized crime.

The Committee on Hemispheric Security meets under the chairmanship of a member state to examine a variety of relevant issues. For example, during its June 4, 2019 meeting, under the chairmanship of Trinidad and Tobago, the committee adopted plans and resolutions to address public security and violence prevention, and a multidimensional approach for advancing hemispheric security.[2]

Unfortunately, preventive diplomacy in the Inter-American region continues to be circumscribed by the powerful United States and its continued practice of the modern variant of the Monroe doctrine. Essentially, this means that a situation can only be dealt with if the United States gives the green light. Diplomacy by other actors is impossible against its objection.

Human rights

The Inter-American Commission and the Inter-American Court on Human Rights have established a solid jurisprudence on the duty of governments to prevent gross violations of human rights. Prominently, in 1968 the commission adopted and transmitted to governments a ground-breaking Resolution on the Protection of Human Rights in Connection with the Suspension of Constitutional Guarantees or the Stage of Siege. The rationale was to stress the duty of governments to prevent violations of human rights. It included significant limitations on a government's ability to suppress civil liberties and other human rights during a suspension of constitutional guarantees accompanying a "state of siege."[3]

In the 1988 Velasquez Rodriguez Case, the court had a superb discussion of the legal duty of governments to prevent human rights violations. The court declared that states have the duty to take reasonable steps to prevent violations and to use the means at their disposal to carry out a serious investigation of violations committed within their jurisdiction, to identify those responsible, to impose the appropriate punishment, and to ensure the victim receives adequate compensation.[4]

This duty to prevent includes all those means of a legal, political, administrative, and cultural nature that promote the protection of human rights and ensure that any violations are considered and treated as illegal acts. However, while states are obligated to prevent human rights abuses, the existence of a particular violation does not, in itself, prove the failure to take preventive measures. On the other hand, subjecting a person to official, repressive bodies

The Americas and Europe 79

that practiced torture and assassination with impunity is itself considered a breach of the duty to prevent violations of the rights to life and physical integrity of the person, even if that particular person is not tortured or assassinated, or if those facts cannot be proven in a concrete case.[5]

In the Velasquez Rodriguez Case, the court also dealt with the duty of states to respect human rights under Article 1 of the Inter-American Convention on Human Rights. The court held that any exercise of public power that violates the rights recognized by the convention is illegal. Any violation of these rights by a state organ or official constitutes a failure of the duty to respect the rights and freedoms set forth in the convention. This conclusion was independent of whether the state had contravened provisions of internal law or overstepped the limits of its authority. Under international law a state was responsible for the acts of its agents undertaken in their official capacity and for their omissions, even when those agents acted outside the sphere of their authority or violated internal law. Furthermore, a state could be held internationally responsible for an illegal act committed by a non-state entity if this was due to a lack of diligence to prevent the violation or to respond to it as required by the convention.[6]

The state has, according to the court, the legal duty to take reasonable steps to prevent human rights violations and to use the means at its disposal to carry out a serious investigation of violations committed within its jurisdiction, to identify those responsible, to impose the appropriate punishment and to ensure the victim adequate compensation.

In the 1999 case of Villagran Morales and others, the court declared in respect of the right to life:

> The right to life is a fundamental human right, and the exercise of this right is essential for the exercise of all other human rights. If it is not respected, all rights lack meaning. Owing to the fundamental nature of the right to life, restrictive approaches to it are inadmissible. In essence, the fundamental right to life includes not only the right of every human being not to be deprived of his life arbitrarily, but also the right that he will not be prevented from having access to the conditions that guarantee a dignified existence. States have the obligation to guarantee the creation of the conditions required in order that violations of this basic right do not occur and, in particular, the duty to prevent its agents from violating it.[7]

In the Velasquez Rodriguez Case the court also affirmed that Article 1 of the convention requires parties to respect the relevant rights and freedoms, and to ensure their free and full exercise without discrimination. In effect, the article was determined to charge states with the fundamental duty to

80 *The Americas and Europe*

respect and guarantee the rights recognized in the convention. The court clarified that the obligation "to ensure" exercise of rights implies a state duty to organize governmental structures so that they are capable of juridically safeguarding human rights. Consequently, states must prevent, investigate, and punish any violation of the relevant rights, and if possible, attempt to restore the right violated and provide compensation.

Climate change, WMDs, democracy, and SDG 16

At its forty-first regular session, held in San Salvador, the OAS General Assembly adopted a resolution on climate change by which member states resolved to: strengthen their resilience to the adverse impacts of climate change, support the development of climate change adaptation activities, support OAS members' efforts to reduce greenhouse gas emissions, and promote capacity building and information exchange related to climate change.

While the OAS has a record of commitment to combating WMDs, there does not seem to be significant preventive diplomacy in this area. Relevant OAS treaties include the Convention on the Prohibition of the Development, Production, Stockpiling and Use of Chemical Weapons and on their Destruction; the Convention on the Prohibition of the Development, Production and Stockpiling of Bacteriological (Biological) and Toxin Weapons and on their Destruction; and the Treaty for the Prohibition of Nuclear Weapons in Latin America and the Caribbean (the Treaty of Tlateloco).

In terms of democracy, the Inter-American Commission on Human Rights, early on, underlined that the right to take part in government and participate in honest, periodic, free elections by secret ballot was of fundamental importance for safeguarding the human rights laid out in the Inter-American human rights instruments. This was because, as historical experience had shown, governments derived from the will of the people, expressed in free elections, were those that provided the soundest guarantee that basic human rights will be observed and protected.[8]

The court has on several occasions clarified the law governing states of siege or emergency in terms that are applicable internationally. In 1985, for example, the court advised that, "[i]n a democratic society, the rights and freedoms inherent in the human person, the guarantees applicable to them and the rule of law form a triad." These are "the principle of legality, democratic institutions and the rule of law."[9]

In an Advisory Opinion on Judicial Guarantees in States of Emergency[10] the court also affirmed that all measures should be proportionate and not exceed the strict limits imposed by the convention. States also have an obligation to provide effective judicial remedies that must be substantiated in accordance with the rules of due process of law. In addition, the opinion

The Americas and Europe   81

stated that the rule of law, representative democracy, and personal liberty are essential in the system for the protection of human rights contained in the convention. It also underlined the importance of the principle of effective judicial remedies to victims of human rights violations.[11]

Lastly, the OAS is advancing inter-agency initiatives that seek the support of member states in the achievement of the SDGs, including SDG 16. The organization's focus, based on its institutional vision and mission of "More Rights for More People," is on equality and social inclusion in the region, which has a direct connection to the promotion of democracy and good governance.[12]

Europe: The OSCE

Historically, the Organization for Security and Cooperation in Europe has been a premier institution when it comes to the exercise of preventive diplomacy. From 1994, the year in which it evolved into an international organization from its predecessor, the Conference on Security and Cooperation in Europe (CSCE), the OSCE dedicated itself to being "a primary instrument for early warning, conflict prevention and crisis management in the region." With a "flexible and dynamic" approach.[13] Diana Chigas, with Elizabeth McClintock and Christophe Kamp, writing two years later, cited several institutions and instruments that would form the cornerstone of the OSCE's preventive diplomacy and conflict management approach: the high commissioner on national minorities, the Permanent Council (the main decision-making body for the day-to-day operations of the OSCE), an expanded role for the chairman-in-office, long-term in-country missions, the role of the OSCE secretary-general, and the Office of Democratic Institutions and Human Rights.[14]

For the past quarter century, the high commissioner has been a pioneering actor in the deployment of preventive diplomacy. ODIHR has also initiated new forms of intercession with a view to heading off crises and conflicts. Unfortunately, as we shall see later in the chapter, like other organizations the OSCE continues to be a victim of its own governments, some powerful, some recalcitrant, many undemocratic, and many oppressive.

Nevertheless, the OSCE has managed to build up a record of pronouncements and some actions on the five themes of interest to us in this book. Its efforts in relation to each is discussed below.

Climate change

Environmental problems, such as climate change, pollution, and the loss of bio-diversity, it has been pointed out, are threatening the security of OSCE

82 *The Americas and Europe*

states and their populations. For example, within the area covered by the organization, every year more than half a million people die prematurely due to air pollution. A growing proportion of this pollution is the result of long-distance transport of air pollutants from other countries.[15] The Helsinki Final Act of 1975 recognized that the protection and improvement of the environment, as well as the protection of nature, is a task of major importance to the well-being of the peoples of, and economic development of, all countries, and that many environmental problems, particularly in Europe, could be solved effectively only through close international cooperation. Much later, in 2007, the OSCE Ministerial Council—the organization's high-level decision-making body—recognized that as a regional security organization under Chapter VIII of the UN Charter, the OSCE has a complementary role to play in addressing this challenge in its region.

The 2003 the OSCE's Strategy Document for the Economic and Environmental Dimension called for strengthening its role by enhancing dialogue among participating states on environmental issues and by improving the review process on the implementation of commitments. To enhance this dialogue, the document stated that the OSCE annual Economic and Environmental Forum should develop a procedure for ensuring follow-up of its deliberations. The forum assesses the implementation of economic and environmental commitments by OSCE states, and identifies priorities for future work.

The OSCE also has an Economic and Environmental Committee (a subsidiary body of the Permanent Council), which meets monthly. In addition, there is an Office of Coordinator of OSCE Economic and Environmental Activities (OCEEA), which supports environmental projects and activities concerning, inter alia, the sustainable use of water, energy security, climate change, and the management of hazardous waste. Furthermore, a network of 60 platforms for dialogue known as Aarhus Centres promotes public participation in environmental decision-making.

Barend ter Haar, a senior research fellow at the Clingendael Institute, argues that the OSCE needs to strengthen its activities in the environmental domain. The secretariat has only been able to make a modest contribution, due to limited means. Instead, fighting the threats of environmental pollution and climate change have to be addressed by states themselves; meanwhile a large number of states are sending passive observers to meetings rather than active participants. Pollution and climate change are a clear and present danger for the security of all OSCE participating states, but so far very few states have sufficiently risen to this challenge. Haar has suggested that the OSCE Network of Think Tanks and Academic Institutions be asked to explore a more dynamic role for the organization.[16]

Weapons of mass destruction

The OSCE has an innovative approach to promoting the non-proliferation of weapons of mass destruction: it helps implement UN Security Council resolution 1540 (2004) on the non-proliferation of weapons of mass destruction, and runs a project that assists interested participating states in producing national action plans and in building up the legislative basis required. The organization also undertakes awareness-raising activities and tailored training, and helps improve legislation, promotes best practices, and intensifies cooperation with other international organizations.[17]

On December 3, 1994 the OSCE adopted a set of principles governing non-proliferation (later updated, on December 4, 2013). These state that the participating governments consider the proliferation of nuclear, chemical, and biological weapons and their means of delivery constitute a threat to international peace, security, and stability. The universalization and reinforcement of the non-proliferation regimes remain a top priority, and participating states committed to preventing proliferation of weapons and delivery vehicles.

The declaration contained measures such as ensuring that participating states' nuclear-related exports do not assist the development of nuclear weapons or other nuclear explosive devices, and that such exports are in full conformity with the objectives and purposes of the 1970 nuclear Non-Proliferation Treaty (NPT). Each participating state also affirms that it will maintain effective security of all nuclear materials and nuclear facilities under their control.

In the principles, states also pledged to support control measures, effective licensing, and enforcement procedures covering the chemical weapons precursors lists, chemical-weapons-related dual-use equipment, and biological-weapon-relevant pathogens and -related dual-use equipment. And to support the effective implementation of the 2002 Hague Code of Conduct against Ballistic Missile Proliferation (HCOC) and universal adherence to it, including its transparency and confidence-building measures. Implementation of the principles is discussed within the OSCE Forum for Security Cooperation.

Conflicts and violence

The OSCE high commissioner on national minorities, a position established a quarter of a century ago, is one of its leading actors for the prevention of conflicts and violence. As the commissioner underlined in a July 2019 address to the International Peace Institute in New York, "My mandate is a conflict prevention mandate."[18] He explained two sides to his work. The first is "quiet diplomacy," which involves watching for instances of ethnic conflict

84　*The Americas and Europe*

and deciding which ones may develop in a dangerous direction, and then engaging with actors and constituencies that could help. The second consists in better informing the public on best practices and lessons learned, "communicating what are things that have worked in other places, and discouraging governments from making policy calls that would create friction." In striving to make societies more peaceful and inclusive, the high commissioner stressed the centrality of integration: "if there are groups not well integrated, there is a high likelihood of seeing marginalization and radicalization and potentially extremism."[19]

Much of the day-to-day work of the office of the high commissioner is in identifying and addressing causes of ethnic tensions and conflicts. The commissioner addresses both short-term triggers of inter-ethnic tension or conflict, and long-term structural concerns. If an OSCE state is not meeting its political commitments or international norms, the commissioner will assist by providing analysis and recommendations. Based on experience, the commissioner also publishes thematic recommendations and guidelines that give advice on common challenges and best practices; and provides structural support through small collaborative projects with the aim of achieving sustainability through increased local ownership.

Countering violent conflict, especially the intra-state and ethnic conflict prevalent today, according to the commissioner in 2019, is *inclusive* policies that help strengthen the cohesiveness of diverse societies and, in turn, their resilience to conflicts and crises. Over the years, the office of high commissioner has developed a set of guidelines and recommendations on a number of policy areas, such as education, the use of language, rule of law, policing, media, participation and inter-state relations for this purpose.

To aid conflict prevention, the office of the high commissioner has established various policies and approaches. One major focus is the role of youth and the importance of balanced policies as tools to promote the full participation of every member of society, including the younger generation, in public life. Education, including language education is the starting point, and requires "quality education for all, with no discrimination against—or self-exclusion by—segments of the population."[20]

For decades the office has also been promoting and supporting integrated and multilingual education in diverse societies, which, the high commissioner argues, has borne promising results in terms of social cohesion. This has involved helping policy-makers achieve a balance between protecting the mother tongue of minorities and the need for minorities to be fluent in the state language(s), in order to be fully engaged in public life and realize their full potential. The office feels that language and education

The Americas and Europe 85

are central to the peace and security agenda, and has promulgated "The Hague Recommendations regarding the Education Rights of National Minorities" and the "Oslo Recommendations regarding the Linguistic Rights of National Minorities." Targeted actions to support youth empowerment have also been carried out, including a youth-driven initiative aimed at ending ethnic segregation.[21]

The office has also conducted activities, for example, in Bosnia-Herzegovina and Serbia to advance the implementation of the 1995 Dayton peace accords (the Dayton Agreement), and has provided support for encouraging the participation of national minorities in Georgia. And since 2014, the office has supported a project to create opportunities for dialogue between political parties and minority representatives. The overall work of the office of the high Commissioner provides a dramatic example of the modern face of contemporary preventive diplomacy in relation to conflicts and violent.

See Box 4.1 below for a May 2019 address by the high commissioner that highlights the role of the media in preventing violence through the protection of national minorities. This discusses the high commissioner's "Tallin Guidelines on National Minorities and the Media in the Digital Age," published in February 2019.

Box 4.1 The Tallin Guidelines: Conflict prevention through protection of national minorities and a focus on the role of the media

Address by OSCE High Commissioner on National Minorities Lamberto Zannier, Vienna, May 23, 2019

The Tallin Guidelines on National Minorities and the Media in the Digital Age emanated from the observation that the fundamental transformations in the media landscape during the past decade have multiplied opportunities to access an abundance of diverse content, as well as tools for individualized and interactive participation in public debate. The ability of media to divulge information and to reach and connect people has been exponentially amplified. So, too has its potential to defuse, or alternatively, ignite conflict. This is particularly relevant for diverse societies, … where minorities and majorities live side by side, the media can offer all groups in society enhanced opportunities to shape their own identities and explore different viewpoints. As media increasingly transcends borders, minorities can easily form transnational networks, which in turn can play a key role in supporting the preservation of cultures and traditions. Regrettably, however, the media also carries risks for peace and stability. Transnational networks involving minorities spread across various States have the potential to interfere in, and

86 The Americas and Europe

possibly damage, bilateral relations. The new media carries the risk of political manipulation, and minorities can be instrumentalized. A rise in inflammatory language in the global political discourse has led to the spread of xenophobic and racist language.

> These Guidelines appeal to the responsibility and the interest of States to ensure that the media and the opportunities it offers are used in a way that minimizes these risks and rather catalyses the integration of diverse societies. The proposed recipe, crystallized in 37 concrete recommendations, is, among others, a mix of multilingualism reflecting the linguistic diversity in society; the participation of various groups, including minorities, in media content production and delivery; and restraint by States in their interference in other countries' affairs. As in other recent Guidelines and Recommendations issued by my Institution, specific attention has been devoted to mainstreaming gender. As such, issues such as the equal participation and representation of women, including those with a minority background, in the media, or protection measures to prevent and counter gender-based violence taking place on these platforms, feature prominently throughout the Tallin Guidelines ...

> Source: Address by OSCE High Commissioner on National Minorities Lamberto Zannier to the OSCE Permanent Council No. 1229, Vienna, May 23, 2019. For the Tallin Guidelines themselves, see: www.osce.org/hcnm/tallinn-guidelines? download=true

Human rights

The OSCE Office for Democratic Institutions and Human Rights is a leading institution of contemporary preventive diplomacy. Established in 1991, it is mandated to assist the 57 OSCE states to "ensure full respect for human rights and fundamental freedoms, to abide by the rule of law, to promote the principles of democracy and ... to build, strengthen and protect democratic institutions, as well as promote tolerance throughout society."[22] All OSCE states have agreed that lasting security cannot be achieved without respect for human rights and functioning democratic institutions, and have committed themselves to a catalog of human rights and democracy norms. These form the basis of what the OSCE calls the human dimension of security.[23]

OSCE states agreed at Helsinki in 1975 to respect human rights and fundamental freedoms, including the freedom of thought, conscience, religion, or belief, for all without distinction as to race, sex, language, or religion. Respect for human rights and fundamental freedoms, democracy, and the rule of law, OSCE states decided at Istanbul in 1999, is also at the core of

The Americas and Europe 87

the OSCE's comprehensive concept of security. They have also agreed to promote the effective exercise of civil, political, economic, cultural, and other rights and freedoms.[24] Human rights and fundamental freedoms are the birthright of all human beings, are inalienable, and are guaranteed by law—and their protection and promotion is the first responsibility of government. Democratic government is based on the will of the people, expressed regularly through free and fair elections. Democracy has as its foundation respect for the human person and the rule of law.[25]

In pursuit of these principles, ODIHR works in five broad areas: promotion of free and fair elections, democratization, human rights, tolerance and non-discrimination, and Roma and Sinti issues. The office observes elections to assess compliance with the OSCE's election-related commitments, and promotes strengthening of the rule of law through assistance in achieving compliance with the organization's commitments regarding judicial independence, access to the legal profession and justice, and criminal justice in general.

ODIHR also fosters democratic governance by providing support to governments in strengthening democratic practices, and carries out human rights training and education activities aimed at raising human rights awareness and enhancing the capacity of civil society to monitor human rights issues. The office also helps governments to combat hate crimes and other violent manifestations of intolerance through, for example, training for law enforcement personnel and strengthening the capacity of civil society to monitor and report on hate crimes. It also promotes freedom of religion or belief through legal reviews and related activities.[26] See Box 4.2 below on recent efforts of the ODIHR in relation to democracy, human rights, and the prevention of violence.

The European Convention on Human Rights dates back to 1950, long before the establishment of the CSCE and the OSCE. It operates under the auspices of the Council of Europe. Nevertheless, it is a key partner to the efforts of the OSCE to advance democracy and human rights and it has developed a significant jurisprudence on the duty of governments to prevent violations of human rights. We set out the salient parts of that jurisprudence later in this section. Before doing so, it would be useful to note the preventive rationale of the 1987 European Convention for the Prevention of Torture.

The European Committee for the Prevention of Torture, a subsidiary body of the Council of Europe, has a mandate from council member states to require aid with carrying out its tasks, including access to territory and the right to travel without restriction, full information on where persons deprived of their liberty are being held, unlimited access to places of detention, and to interview detainees in private. If necessary, the committee may immediately communicate observations to the relevant authorities.

88 *The Americas and Europe*

Box 4.2 ODIHR work in relation to democracy, human rights, and the prevention of violence

Address by Ingibjörg Sólrún Gísladóttir, Director of the OSCE Office for Democratic Institutions and Human Rights, Vienna, March 7, 2019

Intolerance and discrimination continues to be a concern across the OSCE region. Too often, what begins with discrimination and intolerant discourse can escalate into violence and wider scale conflict.

We launched a new programme, the Information Against Hate Crimes Toolkit to strengthen government collection and management of this data. We need to see increased efforts by participating States so we have a more reliable overview of the nature and extent of these horrible crimes throughout our region to make us all in a better position to prevent them and address them when they occur. ODIHR also published a toolkit on a comprehensive approach to countering hate crimes.

Our Office has taken steps to ensure that intolerance is addressed before it degenerates into hate crime. From educational policy guidelines on anti-Semitism published with UNESCO to drafting teaching materials to counter intolerance against Muslims, we believe that working with future generations is a way to ensure a deep impact.

We continued to monitor the human rights situation of Roma and Sinti, including regarding safety and security of their communities. Another area of focus included supporting participation of Roma and Sinti, including of women and youth, in public and political life, which was a special focus of our Third Status Report, reviewing participating States' progress.

As I have said on a number of occasions and feel compelled to continue to repeat, in light of very little overall progress on the situation of Roma and Sinti, participating States must do more to implement their OSCE human dimension commitments and improve the situation of their Roma and Sinti communities. Their situation and the widespread prejudice against them is appalling and the development needs to be reversed. We certainly stand ready to assist and support participating States ...

Election observation remains a high-profile activity of ODIHR. Last year we deployed 16 election-related activities ...

ODIHR continues to not only focus on the technical implementation of electoral commitments, but also on respect for fundamental rights that underpins democratic elections ...

Source: OSCE/ODIHR, "Address by Ingibjörg Sólrún Gísladóttir, Director of the OSCE Office for Democratic Institutions and Human Rights (ODIHR)," 1219th Meeting of the Permanent Council, March 7, 2019, 3–4, www.osce.org/odihr/413534?download=true

The Americas and Europe 89

In the 1976 Handyside Case, the European Court of Human Rights considered as characteristics of a democratic society the notions of pluralism, tolerance, and broad-mindedness. Two years later, in the Klass case, the court considered that one of the fundamental principles of a democracy is the rule of law: justice is best served by constitutional democracy under the rule of law. Then in 2006, in *Zdanoka v. Latvia*, the court captured the relationship between democracy and human rights superbly:

> Democracy constitutes a fundamental element of the "European public order" ... [T]he maintenance and further realization of human rights and fundamental freedoms are best ensured on the one hand by an effective political democracy and on the other by a common understanding and observance of human rights ... European countries have a common heritage of political traditions, ideals, freedom and the rule of law. This common heritage consists in the underlying values of the [European Convention on Human Rights]: thus ... the Convention was in fact designed to maintain and promote the ideals and values of a democratic society. In other words, democracy is the only political model contemplated by the Convention and, accordingly, the only one compatible with it.[27]

In the 2010 case of *Dink v. Turkey*, the court, considering the duty of a government to prevent violations, held that the threat of an assassination had been real and imminent. It held that the Turkish government had a legal responsibility to prevent Firat Dink's assassination, which it had known was being planned.[28]

The jurisprudence of international and regional human rights bodies provides for preventive protection in the event that a potential deportee/extradite would be liable to suffer inhumane treatment, for example political persecution in the country to which they are to be sent, or the death penalty. In the 1989 Soering case, Jens Soering, a German national, was 18 when he and his girlfriend were alleged to have killed her parents in Virginia, a US state that had the death penalty for murder. Soering was subsequently arrested in England and his extradition was sought to the United States. The court ruled that the emotional effect of waiting execution on death row in the United States was a breach of Soering's human rights under the European convention. He could have instead been extradited to Germany, where he would not undergo "suffering of such exceptional intensity or duration."[29]

The court has systematically described the right to vote and stand for election as "central to democracy and the rule of law," thus illustrating the interdependence between these notions. The principle of legality (sometimes

90 *The Americas and Europe*

referred to as supremacy of the law) forms a traditional core aspect of the rule of law concept. The latter requires that the state act on the basis of, and in accordance with, the law. This offers essential legal protection of the individual vis-à-vis the state and its organs and agents. Many ECHR provisions reflect this principle through references to the notion of "law," in most cases in the form of a requirement that interference with human rights must be lawful.[30]

On the principle of lawfulness, the court assesses whether domestic law as a whole has been complied with in the context of interferences with ECHR rights. States are not only obliged to respect and apply, in a foreseeable and consistent manner, the laws they have enacted, but also, as a corollary, to ensure the legal and practical conditions for their implementation.

The court has also held that the principle that all are equal before the law is reflected in various ways in the ECHR, including the prohibition of discrimination. Equality before the law and non-discrimination are human rights principles as much as they are rule of law principles, and the court's case-law tends to apply the prohibition of discrimination without there being a special need to refer to it as a rule of law principle, although there is some recognition that equality in rights and duties of all human beings before the law is an aspect of the rule of law.[31]

The due process aspect of the rule of law also entails certain positive obligations of the state in the form of procedural requirements and safeguards (such as the right to be heard and have one's views considered, e.g. for a pregnant woman concerning the therapeutic termination of her pregnancy). The right of access to a court was also established on the basis of the rule of law principle. The right to a fair trial enshrined in the European convention is another reflection of the fundamental principle of the rule of law.

SDG 16

The OSCE and the European Union are both committed to implementing the SDGs within their member states and abroad, through development cooperation with partner countries. The European answer to the 2030 Agenda includes two work streams. The first track seeks to link the SDGs to the European policy framework and current priorities, assessing where the EU stands and identifying the most relevant sustainability concerns. The second involves reflection work on further developing a longer-term vision and the focus of sectoral policies after 2020. By adopting such a comprehensive approach, the EU seeks to mainstream the SDGs into the work of the European Commission—the day-to-day decision-making body of the EU—and to engage all stakeholders, member states, and the European

The Americas and Europe 91

Parliament in their implementation in order to work toward the full realization of the 2030 Agenda.[32]

Conclusion

In relation to the above discussion on Europe, the OSCE high commissioner on national minorities, ODIHR, and OSCE Visiting Missions have undoubtedly proven their worth as instruments of preventive diplomacy. The former two are models of action that could usefully be emulated in other regions. However, in recent times, the OSCE, like the other organizations discussed in this book, has become victim to its member governments, with the rise of authoritarianism and populism among some.

As stated by its current secretary-general, the OSCE is under challenge and growing constraints. Continuing clashes between Russia and the United States, and the growing presence of China in the region, make it a pawn of global rivalries, and also, the subject of competing ideas of governance. Russia, although a member of OSCE, is an advocate of the sovereign rights of states. China is a practitioner of one-party rule and explicitly and implicitly challenges the norms of the Universal Declaration of Human Rights on which historical OSCE norms of governance have been patterned.

Opportunities for preventive diplomacy in the OSCE area, as indeed in other parts of the world, are increasingly constrained by these global rivalries and clashes of ideas of governance. On top of this, the United States under President Donald Trump has established a commission to reconsider the content of international and national human rights norms -an open challenge to the Universal Declaration of Human Rights. The world, including the OSCE region, is here in treacherous waters for the future of democratic governance under the rule of law and respect for human rights. Without a strong human rights core, it is difficult to see what the future of OSCE preventive diplomacy would be.

In relation to the Americas and the OAS, given that the organization is so heavily under the shadow of the United States, its preventive diplomacy is, unfortunately, largely stultified. It is hard to see member governments frequently acting in defiance of the wishes of the United States, and the OAS's secretary-general and secretariat are similarly constrained. Nevertheless, the organization does, from time to time, engage in useful peacemaking, peacekeeping, and peacebuilding activities.

The Committee on Hemispheric Security is conceptually an innovative body and would fit within the framework of a Global Watch Over Human Security, should this come together, as we argue for in this book. For the time being, however, the committee seems to be just going through the

92 *The Americas and Europe*

motions. The Inter-American Commission and the Inter-American Court of Human Rights have put down a valuable jurisprudence of prevention and, at the time of writing, the commission is known to be engaged in discreet activities behind the scenes in the conflict in Venezuela. But the commission is under attack from powerful governments.

It would be unfortunate, to say the least, if attacks such as these stifle the commission. It has historically been one of the strongest protection actors in the hemisphere, and its jurisprudence of prevention is no less than historic. As we have argued, without genuine respect for, and protection of human rights, preventive diplomacy remains hollow.

Notes

1 See, generally, Adam Isaacson, "Conflict Resolution in the Americas: The Decline of the OAS," *World Politics Review*, May 22, 2012; Osvaldo Kreimer, "Conflict Prevention in the Americas: The Organization of American States," in *Conflict Prevention: Path to Peace of Grand Illusion?* ed. David Carment and Albrecht Schnabel (New York: UN University Press, 2003); and Elizabeth Spehar, "The Role of the Organization of American States in Conflict Prevention," *International Journal on Minority and Group Rights* 8, no. 1 (2001): 61–70.

2 Permanent Council of the OAS, "Hemispheric Plan of Action to Guide the Design of Public Policies to Prevent and Reduce Intentional Homicide," doc. no. CP/CSH-1926/19, June 7, 2019; and OAS, "Advancing Hemispheric Security: A Multidimensional Approach," CP/CSFF-1918/19 rev.3, June 2019. See also Robert Muggah, "Violent Crime Has Undermined Democracy in Latin America," *Financial Times*, July 10, 2019.

3 See Secretariat of the Inter-American Commission on Human Rights, *Inter-American Yearbook on Human Rights, 1968* (Washington, DC: Secretariat of the Inter-American Commission on Human Rights, 1973), 61.

4 Inter-American Court of Human Rights, Velasquez Rodriguez Case, Judgment, July 29, 1988, Ser. C, No. 4, 1988, para.174, http://hrlibrary.umn.edu/iachr/b_11_12d.htm.

5 Ibid., para. 175.

6 Ibid., paras. 170, 172.

7 Inter-American Court of Human Rights, Villagran Morales et al. Case (Case of the "Street Children"), Judgment, November 19, 1999. Available at www.corteidh.or.cr/docs/casos/articulos/seriec_63_ing.pdf.

8 Inter-American Commission on Human Rights, *Ten Years of Activities, 1971–1981* (Washington, DC: OAS, 1982), 334.

9 Inter-American Commission on Human Rights, Advisory Opinion OC-5785, November 13, 1985, Series A, No. 5, para. 66.

10 Inter-American Commission on Human Rights, Advisory Opinion OC-9/87, October 6, 1987, Series A, No. 9.

11 Ibid., para. 24.

12 See International IDEA and Community of Democracies, Inter-Regional Dialogue on Democracy (IRDD), "The Role of Global and Regional Organizations in the Advancement of Sustainable Development Goal 16," Address by the Inter-Parliamentary Union (IPU) Secretary General, Martin

The Americas and Europe   93

Chungong, Geneva, March 13, 2018. Available at www.ipu.org/documents/2018-03/inter-regional-dialogue-democracy-irdd-role-global-and-regional-organizations-in-advancement-sustainable-development-goal-16.

13 CSCE, "Budapest Summit Declaration: Towards a Genuine Partnership in a New Era," doc. no. RC/1/95, December 21, 1994. Available at http://hrlibrary.umn.edu/osce/new/BUDAPEST.htm.

14 Diana Chigas, with Elizabeth McClintock and Christophe Kamp, "Preventive Diplomacy and the Organization for Security and Cooperation in Europe: Creating Incentives for Dialogue and Cooperation," in *Preventing Conflict in the Post-Communist World*, ed. Abram Chayes and Antonia Handler Chayes (Washington, DC: The Brookings Institution, 1996), 37.

15 Barend Ter Haar, "How Should the OSCE Deal with Climate Change and Environmental Threats," Security and Human Rights Monitor, February 19, 2019. Available at www.shrmonitor.org/climate-change-and-security-osce/.

16 Ibid. See also, Lukas Ruettinger, "Climate Change and Security in the OSCE Region: Scenarios for Action and Cooperation," final project report on behalf of the European Environment Agency, OSCE, 2013. Available at www.adelphi.de/en/system/files/mediathek/bilder/climate-change-and-security-in-the-osce-region_osce_eea_adelphi.pdf.

17 See OSCE, "Non-Proliferation of Weapons of Mass Destruction." Available at www.osce.org/forum-for-security-cooperation/107436.

18 International Peace Institute, "OSCE High Commissioner Zannier: Invest in Diversity," July 18, 2019. Available at www.ipinst.org/2019/07/conversation-with-lamberto-zannier-osce-high-commissioner-on-national-minorities.

19 Ibid.

20 OSCE, "Address by Lamberto Zannier, OSCE High Commissioner on National Minorities to the Panel Discussion on 'Preventive Diplomacy in the Changing Landscape of Modern Conflicts: The Role of Regional Organizations,'" United Nations, New York, July 19, 2019, 4. The high commissioner had taken the initiative to gather a number of regional organizations at UN Headquarters to discuss how to capitalize on their different roles and to learn from their respective experiences in conflict prevention, with SDG 16 particularly in mind (that is, promoting peaceful and inclusive societies for sustainable development, providing access to justice for all, and building effective, accountable, and inclusive institutions).

21 Ibid.

22 CSCE, "Helsinki Document 1992: The Challenges of Change," July 9–10, 1992, para. VI(2). Available at www.osce.org/mc/39530?download=true.

23 See OSCE Office for Democratic Institutions and Human Rights. Available at OSCE.org/odihr.

24 CSCE, "Conference on Security and Co-Operation in Europe: Final Act" (the Helsinki Declaration), 1975. Available at www.osce.org/helsinki-final-act?download=true.

25 CSCE, "The Charter of Paris for a New Europe" (the Paris Declaration), Paris, November 19–21, 1990. Available at www.osce.org/mc/39516?download=true.

26 See ODIHR, available at www.osce.org/odihr.

27 European Court of Human Rights, *Zdanoka v. Latvia*, Judgment, March 16, 2006.

28 European Court of Human Rights, *Dink v. Turkey*, Judgment, September 14, 2010.

94 *The Americas and Europe*

29 See Clare Ovey and Robin C. White, *Jacobs & White: The European Convention on Human Rights*, 4th ed. (Oxford University Press, 2006), 101, 103.

30 Council of Europe, European Convention on Human Rights, Protocol No. 1 (1952), Protocol No. 4 (1963), and Protocol No. 7 (1984). See Council of Europe, Search on Treaties. Available at www.coe.int/en/web/conventions/search-on-treaties/-/conventions/treaty/results/subject/3.

31 European Court of Human Rights, *Refah Partisi (the Welfare Party) and Others v. Turkey*, Grand Chamber Judgment, July 31, 2001. The judgment of February 13, 2003 did not refer to equality but to the principle of secularism. The principle of equality before the law is also expressed through specific ECHR requirements concerning judicial proceedings such as equality of arms and impartiality of the judge (Article 6).

32 See International IDEA and Community of Democracies, Inter-Regional Dialogue on Democracy.

5 Conclusion

Optimism about civil society, and a proposed executive preventive role for the UN Security Council

- The role of intergovernmental organizations in contemporary preventive diplomacy
- Civil society actors
- Proposal: An executive preventive role for the UN Security Council

This chapter summarizes findings in relation to the UN and the regional and sub-regional organizations analyzed in the book. It then briefly explores the work of civil society actors before ending with the author's proposal for an executive preventive role for the UN Security Council.

The role of intergovernmental organizations in contemporary preventive diplomacy

The book has argued that the concept of preventive diplomacy has evolved dramatically, and that a modern concept is now in evidence in international relations. Preventive diplomacy currently extends beyond disputes and conflicts to the sensitization of the international community to threats and challenges to the survival and security of humanity. It also encompasses the articulation and pursuit of policies to deal with those threats, and the emplacement of laws and institutions to deal with global issues affecting the welfare of humanity, such as climate change, weapons of mass destruction, disarmament, sustainable development, gross human rights violations, and human security broadly.

The work of the UN and certain regional intergovernmental organizations was examined by exploring evidence in support of the modern concept of preventive diplomacy in relation to five sets of issues: climate change, weapons of mass destruction, conflicts and violence, gross violations of human rights, and the promise of Sustainable Development Goal 16. In the area of climate change, perhaps the most impressive example of contemporary preventive diplomacy is the UN Panel on Climate Change,

96 *Conclusion*

backed by the UN secretary-general and his special envoy for the 2019 Climate Change Summit. The UNPCC has contributed to preventive diplomacy by researching and presenting the facts about global warming, by seeking to mobilize world public opinion about the necessity to change human behavior toward agriculture and husbandry, and about food consumption. Members of the UNPCC have gone on media blitzes to grab the attention of the public and to plead for dramatic changes on many fronts.

However, the most stunning example of preventive diplomacy in the history of international relations has been provided by Greta Thunberg, a 15-year old Swede who has been leading a campaign for action against climate change.[1] Her contribution is discussed along with that of other civil society actors below.

In the area of weapons of mass destruction, a worthwhile continuing effort in contemporary preventive diplomacy is the Comprehensive Nuclear-Test-Ban Treaty (CTBT) organization whose executive secretary and staff engage in various kinds of promotional and reactive preventive diplomacy. The executive secretary and governing body promote contacts and dialogue in instances where it is feared that a state might be about to trigger a nuclear explosion. The CTBT, which is awaiting further ratifications to enter into force, seeks to ban nuclear explosions by everyone, everywhere on the Earth's surface, in the atmosphere, underwater, and underground.[2]

When it comes to conflicts and violence, a spectacular example of contemporary preventive diplomacy is the work of the OSCE high commissioner on national minorities. We saw how the high commissioner seeks to tackle short-term and long-term causes of ethnic tensions and to promote inclusiveness through educational and language programs. The AU Panel of the Wise is another example of solid contemporary preventive diplomacy. Members of the panel, collectively or individually, help conciliate difficult situations with a view to heading off their deterioration into conflict. Useful preventive diplomacy is also carried out by the UN regional centers in Central Africa, West Africa/North Africa, and Central Asia.

The conflict prevention efforts of the UN Department of Political and Peacebuilding Affairs, the UN Development Programme (UNDP), and that of the African organizations discussed in Chapter 2—the AU, ECOWAS, IGAD, and SADC—are noteworthy and there is much imaginative contemporary preventive diplomacy to be seen in their activities. IGAD, for example, specializes in the prevention of climate-related conflicts such as expanding deserts and the movement of herding communities onto the lands of farming communities.

DPPA and UNDP run a helpful program that has provided political/development advisers to some 60 countries thus far. The latter promotes and facilitates the role of local mediators with knowledge of local conditions,

Conclusion 97

and its Crisis Bureau helps to build up national infrastructures for crisis prevention in the aftermath of natural and man-made disasters. See Box 5.1 below for a summary of some preventive activities in 2018 by DPPA (which was until then known as DPA).

In Asia, ASEAN has historically been a useful actor engaging in preventive diplomacy, and its Regional Forum provides an opportunity for member states and external powers to review wider Asian problems. Unfortunately, ASEAN seems to have lost steam in recent years and is in need of revitalization in this area. More hopefully, its Intergovernmental Commission on Human Rights has been addressing underlying causes of conflicts and thereby makes a modest contribution.

In the Americas, the OAS has an interesting Committee on Hemispheric Security, but its actual vitality seems in doubt. It has historically

---

Box 5.1 Preventive engagements in 2018 by the UN Department of Political Affairs (now DPPA)

The Horn of Africa: the DPA conducted various initiatives with governments and regional organizations, including providing capacity-building training in mediation and negotiation to young Egyptian, Eritrean, and Ethiopian diplomats.

Central and West Africa: in Sierra Leone, UN Special Representative Mohamed Ibn Chambas coordinated with ECOWAS to encourage the holding of credible, peaceful elections. In Cameroon, Special Representative Francois Lounceny Fall made several visits to similarly help facilitate elections, and to engage in discussions on how to deal with the situation in the North-West and South-West regions of the country.

Central Asia: the United Nations Regional Centre for Preventive Diplomacy engaged with stakeholders to facilitate the creation of a solution to conflicts over trans-boundary water management (which have had a significant impact on stability in the region).

Central America: in El Salvador, at the request of the government, DPA facilitated political dialogue among parliamentary political parties. In Honduras, also at the request of the government, a senior mediation adviser was sent by DPA to explore the possibility of future dialogue; this led to the recommendation of a series of confidence-building measures.

Source: DPA, "DPA 2018 Annual Report: Multi-Year Appeal," 2018, 9–11, https://dppa.un.org/sites/default/files/2018_annual_report_of_the_multi-year_appeal_website.pdf. In January 2019, the Department of Political Affairs (DPA) and the Department of Peacekeeping Operations (DPKO) merged to become the Department of Political and Peacebuilding Affairs (DPPA)

98 *Conclusion*

been in the shadow of the US colossus and remains so. In Europe, the OSCE, along with its high commissioner on national minorities, makes a useful contribution through its country missions. In the area of human rights, the OSCE's ODIHR stands out. Its work in democracy promotion, observance of elections, and promotion of human rights is often helpful in preventing the deterioration of tense situations.

Other bodies, such as the UN Human Rights Council, the Office of UN High Commissioner for Human Rights, and regional human rights bodies such as the African Commission on Human and Peoples' Rights, the ASEAN Intergovernmental Commission on Human Rights, and the Inter-American Commission on Human Rights may make the occasional contribution to preventive diplomacy but there is mostly a void to be filled on the part of all of these human rights bodies.

Sustainable Development Goal 16, which is dedicated to the promotion of peace, justice, and strong institutions, has so far had negligible impact in the promotion of preventive policies and strategies. This is largely because governments have so far not been ready to address issues of governance and human rights, without which SDG 16 in its essence cannot be achieved.

Perhaps more hopefully, some nongovernmental actors have engaged in significant preventive work, including preventive diplomacy. Much of this work provides optimism for the future and a few prominent examples are discussed next. The chapter ends by presenting the author's proposal for an executive preventive role for the UN Security Council.

Civil society actors

A 15-year-old Swede, Greta Thunberg, emerged on the world scene in 2018 as the most spectacular example of individual preventive diplomacy ever seen in the history of international relations, sparking a worldwide campaign by schoolchildren calling for action against climate change. As she explains in *No One Is Too Small to Make a Difference*, in 2018 Thunberg wrote an essay on climate change that was published in a Swedish newspaper. The essay attracted a great deal of interest but, as she explains, no one was willing to take practical action. So, she decided to take time off from school and to do a one-person protest outside the Swedish Parliament.

Her protest action inspired other Swedish schoolchildren, and then similar action by others worldwide. She herself has become an articulate champion of action against climate change, making speeches at a number of important institutions worldwide. On the eve of the UN Climate Action Summit in September 2019, Thunberg inspired some 4 million young people worldwide to rally in favor of action to reverse climate change. She made a dramatic address to the summit that galvanized attention worldwide. The past was engaging with the future. If any one person has galvanized world attention on the need to act on climate change, it is this schoolgirl. She is engaging in public, preventive diplomacy by an individual of a kind never seen before. She is the face of contemporary preventive diplomacy. See Box 5.2 below for a transcript of Thunberg's speech to the UN General Assembly in September 2019.

Next, the work of the following prominent nongovernmental organizations and other civil society initiatives is briefly examined: the Worldwatch

---

Box 5.2 Greta Thunberg's address at the UN Climate Action Summit, September 23, 2019

My message is that we'll be watching you.

This is all wrong. I shouldn't be here. I should be back in school on the other side of the ocean. Yet you all come to us young people for hope. How dare you!

You have stolen my dreams and my childhood with your empty words. And yet I'm one of the lucky ones. People are suffering. People are dying. Entire ecosystems are collapsing. We are at the beginning of a mass extinction, and all you can talk about is money and fairy tales of eternal economic growth. How dare you!

For more than 30 years, science has been crystal clear. How dare you continue to look away and come here saying that you're doing enough, when the politics and solutions needed are still nowhere in sight.

You say you hear us and that you understand the urgency. But no matter how sad and angry I am, I do not want to believe that. Because if you really understood the situation and still kept on failing to act, then you would be evil. And that I refuse to believe.

The popular idea of cutting our emissions in half in 10 years only gives us a 50% chance of staying below 1.5 degrees (Celsius), and the risk of setting off irreversible chain reactions beyond human control.

Fifty percent may be acceptable to you. But those numbers do not include tipping points, most feedback loops, additional warming hidden by toxic air pollution or the aspects of equity and climate justice. They also rely on my generation sucking hundreds of billions of tons of your CO_2 out of the air with technologies that barely exist.

So a 50% risk is simply not acceptable to us—we who have to live with the consequences.

To have a 67% chance of staying below a 1.5 degrees global temperature rise—the best odds given by the Intergovernmental Panel on Climate Change—the world had 420 gigatons of CO_2 left to emit back on January 1st, 2018. Today that figure is already down to less than 350 gigatons.

How dare you pretend that this can be solved with just "business as usual" and some technical solutions? With today's emissions levels, that remaining CO_2 budget will be entirely gone within less than eight and a half years.

100 Conclusion

> There will not be any solutions or plans presented in line with these figures here today, because these numbers are too uncomfortable. And you are still not mature enough to tell it like it is.
> You are failing us. But the young people are starting to understand your betrayal. The eyes of all future generations are upon you. And if you choose to fail us, I say, "We will never forgive you."
> We will not let you get away with this. Right here, right now is where we draw the line. The world is waking up. And change is coming, whether you like it or not.
> Thank you.
>
> Source: NPR, "Transcript: Greta Thunberg's Speech at The UN Climate Action Summit," September 23, 2019, www.npr. org/2019/09/23/763452863/transcript-greta-thunbergs-speech-at-the-u-n-climate-action-summit

Institute, the International Institute of Strategic Studies (IISS), the Stockholm International Peace Research Institute (SIPRI), Survival International, the International Crisis Group, International Alert, Anti-Slavery International (ASI), Minority Rights Group International, World Organization Against Torture (OMCT), the Association for the Prevention of Torture (APT), the Global Centre for the Responsibility to Protect, The Elders, and the African Centre for the Constructive Resolution of Disputes (ACCORD). They all engage in significant preventive work, including preventive diplomacy.

The mission of the Worldwatch Institute, an independent research organization, is to generate and promote insights and ideas that empower decision-makers to build an ecologically sustainable society that meets human needs. Operating since 1974, the institute's research is based on the best available evidence and focuses on the challenges that climate change, resource degradation, and population growth pose for meeting human needs in the twenty-first century. Worldwatch seeks solutions to intractable problems that emphasize a blend of government leadership, private sector enterprise, and citizen action. The organization has been warning since at least 1981 that our escalating food demands are leading to topsoil losses that are eroding the foundations of civilization itself; and that deforestation, overgrowing, and overfishing are shrinking the economy's resource base.[3]

The International Institute of Strategic Studies is an internationally renowned British-based international affairs think tank. Founded in 1958, it seeks to be a primary source of accurate, objective information on international strategic issues for politicians and diplomats, foreign affairs analysts, international business, economists, the military, defense commentators,

Conclusion 101

journalists, academics, and the public. It generates various publications relevant to preventive diplomacy, including the Military Balance, an annual assessment of nations' military capabilities; the Armed Conflict Database; *Survival*, a journal on global politics and strategy; *Strategic Survey*, an annual review of world affairs; the Adelphi Papers series of monographs; and Strategic Comments, an online analysis of topical issues in international affairs.

The Stockholm International Peace Research Institute, established in 1966, is an independent international institute for research into problems of peace and conflict, especially those of arms control and disarmament. The SIPRI Yearbook was first published in 1969. This presents a combination of original data in areas such as world military expenditure, international arms transfers, arms production, nuclear forces, major armed conflicts, and multilateral peace operations. SIPRI's current research program centers on: armed conflicts and conflict management; arms transfers; Euro-Atlantic, regional, and global security; military expenditure and arms production; non-proliferation and export control; arms control and disarmament documentation survey; and IT projects, including the FIRST (Facts on International Relations and Security Trends) online database.

Survival International, in operation since 1969, supports tribal peoples worldwide. It does this in three complementary ways: through education, advocacy, and campaigns. It also offers tribal people themselves a platform to address the world. The organization also works closely with local indigenous organizations, and focuses on tribal peoples who have the most to lose, usually those most recently in contact with the outside world.

The International Crisis Group, operating since 1995, is a leading independent source of analysis and advice on conflict prevention to governments and intergovernmental bodies like the United Nations, the European Union, and the World Bank on the prevention and resolution of deadly conflict. The organization's reports provide some of the most valuable alerts about impending conflicts and suggestions as to how they may be prevented.

International Alert was established by Martin Ennals to help prevent gross violations of human rights. In its early years it did useful behind-the-scenes work in places such as the Philippines and Uganda. Later it became active in situations in places such as Sri Lanka and Sierra Leone. Currently it presents itself as an independent peacebuilding organization working directly with people affected by violent conflict and government, at the EU and the UN to shape policy and practice in building sustainable peace. It works to strengthen the expertise, impact, and public profile of the peacebuilding sector. It also organizes training courses and publishes resources on peacebuilding.

102 *Conclusion*

Anti-Slavery International, founded in 1839, is the world's oldest international human rights organization working exclusively against slavery and related abuses. It works at the local, national, and international levels to eliminate the system of slavery around the world by urging governments of countries with slavery to develop and implement measures to end it. ASI also lobbies governments and intergovernmental agencies to make slavery a priority issue, supports research to assess the scale of slavery in order to identify measures to end it, works with local organizations to raise public awareness of slavery, and educates the public about the realities of slavery and campaigns for its end.

Minority Rights Group International works to secure rights for ethnic, religious, and linguistic minorities, and indigenous people around the world. It works with minority communities, providing education and training to enable them to claim their rightful place in society. The organization also lobbies governments and the UN alongside and on behalf of minorities. In addition, it publishes authoritative reports that are widely valued by academics and journalists, while its pioneering legal cases program is advancing the protection of minorities under international law.

The World Organization Against Torture was established in 1986 as a coalition of international NGOs fighting against torture, summary executions, enforced disappearances, and other cruel, inhuman, and degrading treatment. With 282 affiliated organizations in its SOS Torture Network and many tens of thousands of correspondents in every country, OMCT coordinates a network working for the protection of human rights around the world. OMCT's international secretariat provides personalized medical, legal, and social assistance to hundreds of torture victims and ensures the daily dissemination or urgent appeals across the world in order to protect individuals and to fight against impunity.

The Association for the Prevention of Torture has worked since 1977 for a world in which no one is subjected to torture or other cruel, inhuman, or degrading treatment or punishment. The APT has campaigned for the entry into force and effective implementation of the Optional Protocol to the UN Convention against Torture (OPCAT), an international legal instrument that seeks to open all places of detention to international and national scrutiny. The APT also provides training, legal advice, and practical tools, facilitating exchanges and advocating for preventive measures and mechanisms.

Global Centre for the Responsibility to Protect, was established in 2008 by key supporters from government, NGOs, and academia to ensure that the "responsibility to protect" doctrine is understood and put into practice by governments and at the UN. Its mission is to promote and catalyze international action to help countries to prevent or halt mass atrocities.

Conclusion 103

The Elders, a group set up by Nelson Mandela and now headed by Mary Robinson, is an organization that focuses on areas where they consider they can make a difference. This can mean engaging in private advocacy, using their collective influence to open doors and gain access to decision-makers. At other times, The Elders work publicly to promote neglected issues and speak out against injustice by promoting dialogue, providing an independent voice, challenging injustice and breaking taboos, amplifying and supporting the work of people affected by conflict or working for peace, and creating space for campaigners and policy makers to broach difficult issues.[4] They have engaged in considerable efforts to help stop the conflict in Syria and to promote peaceful elections in Zimbabwe. See Box 5.3 below for details on the latter.

The African Centre for the Constructive Resolution of Disputes works throughout Africa to bring creative African solutions to the challenges posed by conflict on the continent. Operating since 1992 and based in South Africa, ACCORD works across the peacemaking–peacekeeping–peacebuilding continuum as it seeks to encourage and promote the constructive resolution of

---

Box 5.3 Elders support democratic transition in Zimbabwe via a letter to SADC

The Elders ... have urged the heads of state of the Southern African Development Community (SADC) to support Zimbabwe through an upcoming transitional period.

In a letter to the SADC, they point out that Zimbabwe is "on the verge of an important transition." The advocates behind the letter, including Kofi Annan, Graca Machel and Archbishop Desmond Tutu, note that with the support of the SADC, Zimbabwe could experience a shift to democratic leadership and a boost to their economic and social development ...

The Elder's letter comes at an auspicious time considering the current tumult within Zimbabwe. Additionally, the letter prefaces the upcoming SADC group summit in Swaziland.

In the letter, not only do the Elders support Zimbabwe, but they also make clear that aid to Zimbabwe will be beneficial for the nation as a whole and should, therefore, be something that SADC thoroughly consider in their impending meeting.

The letter states, "The Elders believe the upcoming summit is an important opportunity to reflect on how best SADC can help Zimbabwe manage the complex challenges ahead."

Source: The Borgen Project, "The Elders Support Zimbabwe through a Letter to SADC," November 6, 2016, https://borgenproject.org/the-elders-support-zimbabwe/

104 *Conclusion*

disputes in Africa and to assist in achieving political stability, economic recovery, and peaceful co-existence within just and democratic societies. In doing so, the organization focuses on encouraging and consolidating dialogue toward the prevention, management, and transformation of conflict. This work is underpinned by in-depth research and knowledge production.[5]

The principles underpinning its operation are peaceful resolution of conflict, human rights, and good governance. Since 1992, ACCORD has played an integral role in conflict resolution activities across Africa. In the fields of conflict prevention, resolution, and management, it intercedes through mediation, negotiation, and training activities. In 2019, the UN Security Council, discussing the maintenance of international peace and security, invited the executive director of ACCORD to address it and share the organization's insights.

The discussion of the work of these organizations has registered that contemporary preventive diplomacy takes dynamic forms and involves not only classical diplomatic activities of governments, and international and regional organizations, but also individual efforts as well as those of civil society groups to help alert the world to dangers threatening the survival of humanity as a whole or of particular groups in danger. Civil society actors also engage in efforts to prevent gross violations of human rights and to help protect people undergoing such violations. Contemporary preventive diplomacy is thus very much peoples' diplomacy as well as that of governments, and international and regional organizations.

Proposal: An executive preventive role for the UN Security Council

The UN Security Council remains, for the most part, a reactive body. Admittedly, when it reacts to some crises this might have a preventive effect. It is our submission that there is need for a profound change in the role of the Security Council to transform it into an executive organ watching over the welfare of humanity and engaging in stronger preventive diplomacy. It is only thus that it can become a truly preventive body. We are aware of the political complications surrounding the work of the Security Council and we leave aside for the moment issues such as reform of its membership. In our view, one has to compartmentalize consideration of its executive role and reform of its membership. We must deal with the council as it exists for the time being.

Let us explain what we consider to be the executive role that the council must play in the future if it is to contribute meaningfully to international security and preventive diplomacy. In the third edition of *The Charter of the United Nations: A Commentary*, the authors note that the

Conclusion 105

threats to peace and security in the twenty-first century include not just international war and conflict, but civil violence, organized crime, terrorism, and weapons of mass destruction. They also include poverty, deadly infectious disease, and environmental degradation since these can have equally catastrophic consequences. All of these threats can cause death or lessen life chances on a large scale, and can undermine states as the basic unit of the international system.[6]

The term "international security" requires in turn:

> a transformation of international relations so that every State is assured that peace will not be broken, or at least that any breach of the peace will be limited in its impact. International security implies the right of every State to take advantage of any relevant security system, while also implying the legal obligations of every State to support such systems.

The General Assembly has stated that national and international security have become increasingly interrelated, which accordingly makes it necessary for states to approach international security in a comprehensive and cooperative manner.[7]

What do the changing threats to international security signify for the future of international law and order, and for the future role of the UN Security Council? Nick Butler, visiting professor and chair of the Kings Policy Institute at Kings College London, has argued that climate "change" sounds too mild a description and implies a gradual, linear shift over decades to temperatures two degrees higher than we are used to. The more likely reality, however, is climate disruption—erratic shifts in one direction or another. These raise the need for what the French government calls "green defense" in the face of threats such as greater levels of migration and faster spreading epidemics, which require European governments to take action outside the region. The French have begun to perceive climate change as a defense and security challenge.[8]

Martin Rees, the British Astronomer Royal, has also argued that while we need to utilize the knowledge of scientists, to deal with the catastrophic potential consequences of climate change, successful implementation of ideas requires "the full commitment of political leaders and the full support of the voting public."[9]

On February 2, 2011, former UN Secretary-General Ban Ki-moon delivered the fourth Cyril Foster Lecture at Oxford University on the topic of "Human Protection and the United Nations in the Twenty-First Century." He noted that the founders of the UN had understood that sovereignty confers responsibility, a responsibility to ensure protection of human beings from

106 *Conclusion*

want, war, and repression. When that responsibility is not discharged, the international community is morally obliged to consider its duty to act in the service of human protection.

"The challenges facing us," he acknowledged,

> have changed, but our core responsibility to maintain international peace and security has not. Slowly but surely, sometimes by trial and error, we have learned to use the instruments available under the Charter in new ways, adapting to evolving circumstances. Through this evolution, the need to operationalize a concept of human protection has emerged.

He went on to say that the UN needs to perform its protection duties more effectively: the best form of protection is prevention—prevention saves lives as well as resources.

Ban Ki-moon argued that beyond the immediate protection agenda the UN is addressing "creeping vulnerabilities," which put populations at risk, weaken societies, and plant the seeds of violence and conflict: they include water scarcity, food insecurity, corruption, transnational crime, and the effects of climate change. Water scarcity, itself worsened by climate change, has become a source of various serious regional conflicts. Therefore, it is not surprising that such human security issues are finding their way onto the peacebuilding agenda, and specifically that of the UN Peacebuilding Commission. He acknowledged that the UN "recognizes that human protection stands at the centre of both its purposes and principles."

The UN will have to change its approaches dramatically if it is to rise to the challenges of international protection. This will require great daring. In his acclaimed book *World Order*, Henry Kissinger observed that:

> the idea that ... countries will identify violations of peace identically and be prepared to act in common against them is belied by the experience of history ... Collective security has repeatedly revealed itself to be unworkable in situations that most seriously threaten international peace and security.[10]

However, Kissinger did not factor into his thinking the changing challenges of international security and human protection. The contemporary and future threats to international security and the challenges of international protection are such that even the mighty powers will have to recognize that UN action is necessary to save humanity and its habitat.

We shall need to turn to the UN as a system of public order,[11] which will require the transformation of international law into a law of international

Conclusion 107

security and protection. The foundations for this are already in place. They consist of:

- The competences of the Security Council under Chapter 7 of the UN Charter: the Security Council must transform itself into the world's "Executive Authority";
- The competences of the UN secretary-general under Article 99 of the Charter: the secretary-general must increasingly make submissions, including legal ones, to the Security Council under Article 99 and invite it to issue mandatory orders under Chapter 7;
- The recommendatory competences of the General Assembly combined with the process of the formation of international customary law: the secretary-general must use his Annual Reports to the General Assembly to draw its attention to threats to human security and to indicate policies and recommendations that can, through widespread consensus, crystallize into norms of international customary law; and
- The interpretative role of the International Court of Justice to clarify the role of the law in meeting the circumstances of contemporary society: the Security Council and General Assembly should use their competences to submit requests to the International Court of Justice for advisory opinions on the duties of states to cooperate for the security and protection of humanity and its habitat.

There is also room for:

- Security advisories by heads of UN agencies;
- Protection alerts by the UN high commissioner for human rights; and
- Security and protection actions by regional organizations.

The urgent need for progressive development of international law in key areas has also been identified by scholars and practitioners. Ken Conca encourages the international community to urgently:

- Find an explicit human right to a safe and healthy environment;
- Acknowledge an environmental "responsibility to protect";
- Infuse the law-and-development approach with stronger peace-and rights practice;
- Find a legitimate (and clearly limited) environmental role for the Security Council;
- Exploit opportunities for environmental peacebuilding; and
- Reconceive and strengthen what it means for the UN to make a "system-wide" response to environmental problems.[12]

108 *Conclusion*

How is the international community to proceed in this reconceptualizing of international security and international law to meet the new challenges of security and human protection? The place to start would be for the Security Council to hold an urgent debate on the need for a new international law of security and protection. An enlightened member of the council could submit a concept paper and advocate such a debate.

Notes

1 Greta Thunberg, *No One Is Too Small to Make a Difference* (London: Penguin, 2019).
2 See CTBTO Preparatory Commission, "CTBT: Ending Nuclear Explosions." Available at www.ctbto.org/fileadmin/user_upload/public_information/CTBT_ Ending_Nuclear_Explosions_web.pdf.
3 Lester R. Brown, *Building a Sustainable Society* (New York, W.W. Norton, 1981.
4 See The Elders, "Who We Are." Available at https://theelders.org/who-we-are.
5 See ACCORD, "ACCORD's Work," www.accord.org.za/about/our-work/.
6 Bruno Simma, Daniel-Erasmus Khan, Georg Nolte, and Andreas Paulus, ed. *The Charter of the United Nations: A Commentary*, 3rd ed., Vol. I (Oxford, University Press, 2012), 111–112.
7 Ibid.
8 Nick Butler, "Action on Climate Change Is Self-Defence Not Altruism," *Financial Times*, October 20, 2015.
9 Martin Rees, "Scientists and Politicians Alike Must Rally to Protect Life on Earth," *Financial Times*, September 5–6, 2015.
10 Henry Kissinger, *World Order* (New York: Penguin Press, 2014), 262–265.
11 Ian Brownlie, *Principles of Public International Law*, 6th ed. (Oxford University Press, 2003), 706.
12 Ken Conca, *An Unfinished Foundation: The United Nations and Global Environmental Governance* (Oxford University Press, 2015).

Select bibliography

Al Khalili, ed., Jim, *What's Next?* (London: Profile Books, 2017). Contains riveting chapters on the future of the planet, the future of us, the future online, marking the future, and the far future.

Andrews, John, *The World in Conflict: Understanding the World's Troublespots* (London: The Economist, 2017). Discusses underlying causes of conflicts and provides a useful survey, region by region, of trouble spots that have seen conflicts or could do in the future.

Boutros-Ghali, Boutros, *An Agenda for Peace* (New York: United Nations, 1992). A seminal report setting out strategies of preventive diplomacy for the United Nations.

Chayes, Abram and Chayes, Antonia Handler, eds., *Preventing Conflict in the Post-Communist World* (Washington, DC: The Brookings Institution, 1996). Contains a good historical discussion of the role of the OSCE in engaging in preventive diplomacy.

Independent Commission on Regional Security Architecture, "Preserving the Long Peace in Asia: The Institutional Building Blocks of Long-Term Regional Security," Asia Society Policy Institute, New York, September 2017. Available at https://asiasociety.org/policy-institute/preserving-long-peace-asia. An invaluable discussion of the need to strengthen institutions for the prevention of conflict in Asia and the Pacific.

Kissinger, Henry A., *Diplomacy* (New York: Simon & Schuster, 1994). A good historical discussion of the role of diplomacy in international affairs.

Mahubani, Kishore and Sng, Jeffery, *The ASEAN Miracle: A Catalyst for Peace* (Singapore: Ridge Books, 2017). Discusses the history of the ASEAN region and has helpful chapters on the ASEAN "ecosystem of peace," and ASEAN and the great powers.

Makinda, Samuel M., Okumu, F. Walufa, and Mickler, David, *The African Union: Addressing the Challenges of Peace, Security and Governance*, 2nd ed. (London: Routledge, 2016). Provides insights into the challenges of preventive diplomacy in Africa.

Ramcharan, Bertrand, *Preventive Diplomacy at the United Nations* (Bloomington: Indiana University Press, 2008). Provides background on the history of preventive diplomacy at the United Nations.

110 *Select bibliography*

Rudd, Kevin, "The Avoidable War: Reflections on US-China Relations and the End of Strategic Engagement," Asia Society Policy Institute, New York, January 2019. Contains a selection of the speeches of Kevin Rudd, former prime minister of Australia and president of the Asia Society Policy Institute, on strategies for preventing war between China and the United States.

Sachs, Jeffrey D., *The Age of Sustainable Development* (New York: Columbia University Press, 2015). A superb discussion of the economic and social conditions affecting the realization of the UN Sustainable Development Goals. Of particular relevance is information on the implementation of SDG 16 (on development, peace, justice, and equitable and strong societies).

United Nations and World Bank, "Pathways for Peace: Inclusive Approaches to Preventing Violent Conflict," The World Bank, Washington, DC, 2018. Offers new ideas for UN preventive diplomacy anchored in the implementation of the Sustainable Development Goals.

Index

Aarhus Centres 82
Action Towards Climate-Friendly
    Transport Initiative 12
Addis Ababa 53
Afghanistan 18, 19–20
Africa 42–58, 103–104; civil society in
    20, 47, 48, 53, 103–104; and climate
    change 43–44, 96; conflicts and
    violence in 50–56, 103, 104;
    democracy in 43, 46, 54, 56,
    103–104; human rights in 18, 20,
    56–57, 98; minorities in 5–6, 49, 57;
    see also individual countries
Africa Regional Strategy on Disaster
    Risk Reduction (DRR) 43
African Centre for the Constructive
    Resolution of Disputes (ACCORD)
    99–100, 103–104
African Charter on Human and
    Peoples' Rights 49–50
African Commission on Human and
    Peoples' Rights 48, 49, 56, 57
African Commission on Nuclear
    Energy (AFONE) 44, 47
African Development Bank 50
African Nuclear-Weapons-Free Zone
    Treaty 44
African Peer Review Mechanism
    (APRM) 50
African Strategy on Meteorology
    (Weather and Climate Services) 43
African Union (AU) 4, 5, 6, 16, 20, 37,
    42–50, 55, 56, 96; climate change
    42–44, 55; conflicts and violence
    42–43, 45, 46–48, 49, 56, 96; human

rights 4, 5–6, 42–43, 45, 46, 48–50,
    57; Panel of the Wise 42, 47–48, 56,
    96; Peace and Security Council 5,
    46, 47; and SDG 16, 42–43, 50, 56;
    Silencing the Guns 45, 51; and the
    UN 45–46, 47, 50, 51–52; and
    WMDs 42–43, 44–46
Agenda 2030 (UN) 4, 36, 50, 64, 90–91
Agenda 2063 (AU) 44, 50
An Agenda for Peace 1, 15
Al Qaeda 76
Americas 91, 97–98; democracy in 76,
    77, 80–81; see also Latin America;
    Organization of American States
    (OAS)
Aminga, Vane Moraa 43
Angola 17
Annan, Kofi 32, 103
Anti-Slavery International (ASI)
    99–100, 102
Arab League 5, 6, 59, 65, 66–67
Arab Spring 48
Arctic 10, 11
Arias, Oscar 76
ASEAN Intergovernmental
    Commission on Human Rights
    (AICHR) 62, 63, 72, 97, 98
ASEAN Regional Forum (ARF) 5, 61,
    71, 97
ASEAN Socio-Cultural Community
    (ASCC) Blueprint 2025 60
ASEAN Working Group on Climate
    Change (AWGCC) 60
Asia 5, 6, 22, 59–75; Central Asia 16,
    17–18, 19–20, 21, 69, 96, 97; civil

112 *Index*

Asia *continued*
society in 21, 61–62; conflicts and
violence in 65–68, 72–73;
democracy in 62, 64, 65; East Asia
16, 45; human rights in 19, 72, 91;
minorities in 6, 62, 72; West Asia 16;
see also Arab League; Association of
Southeast Asian Nations (ASEAN)
Asia Cooperation Dialogue (ACD) 59,
66, 67–68, 70
Asia Society Policy Institute 66, 72, 73
Association for the Prevention of
Torture (APT) 99–100, 102
Association of Southeast Asian Nations
(ASEAN) 4, 37, 59–65, 71–72, 97;
climate change 60, 63; conflicts and
violence 61–62, 71, 97; human rights
5, 59, 62, 63–64, 72, 97, 98; and
SDG 16, 64–65, 72; and WMDs
60–61, 72
Australia 70, 71

Bahrain 67
"Bali Principles" 71
Ban Ki-moon 105–106
Bangkok Treaty 61
Bangladesh 67
Bangsamoro Organic Law 65
al-Bashir, Omar 56
Beijing 68
Benin 18, 20
Bindoff, Nathan 10
biological weapons 3, 60, 80, 83
birth registrations 35, 37, 65
Bogota, Pact of (Inter-American Treaty
on Pacific Settlement 1948) 76, 77
Boko Haram 17
Bosnia 24, 85
Boutros-Ghali, Boutros 15
Burkina Faso 11, 18, 20
Burundi 17
Butler, Nick 105

Cambodia 24, 60, 61, 71
Cameroon 11, 17, 97
Central Africa 16, 17, 96, 97
Central African Forest Initiative 12
Central African Republic (CAR) 17,
48, 51, 52–53
Central America 75, 76, 97

Central Asia 16, 17–18, 19–20, 21, 69,
96, 97
Chad 11, 17, 50, 52–53
Ibn Chambas, Mohamed 97
Charter of the United Nations 8, 9, 15,
16, 22, 23, 29, 61, 82, 104–105,
106, 107
chemical weapons 3, 60, 80, 83
Chigas, Diana 81
children 20, 35, 37, 47; *see also* young
people
China 10, 59, 65–66, 67, 68, 70–72, 73,
76, 91
city planning 12
civil society 6, 11, 12, 14, 22, 32, 62,
69, 87, 98–104; in Africa 20, 47, 48,
53, 103–104; in Asia 21, 61–62;
conflicts and violence 101, 103; and
SDG 16, 4, 8, 34, 35–36, 37
Climate Action Summit (2019) 10,
11–12, 98–100
climate change 1, 2–3, 4, 95–96,
98–100, 105, 106; and Africa 43–44,
96; and ASEAN 60, 63; and the AU
42–44, 55; and conflicts and violence
2, 10–11, 13, 56, 105, 106; and the
OAS 75–76, 80; and the OSCE
81–82; and the UN 2–3, 8–9, 10–13,
38, 95–96; *see also* global warming
Climate for Development in Africa
program on Climate for Development
in Africa (ClimDEV-Africa) 43
CO_2 emissions 43, 99
Coady, Allison Marie 55
Cold War 2, 13, 25, 27
Collective Security Treaty Organization
(CSTO) 68, 69
Colombia 22
colonialism 55
Commission on Human Rights 28, 31, 33
Committee on Hemispheric Security 5,
75, 77, 78, 91–92, 97–98
Common Market for Eastern and
Southern Africa (COMESA) 53
Commonwealth of Independent States
(CIS) 22, 68, 69
Community of Sahel-Saharan States
(CEN-SAD) 52–53
Comprehensive Nuclear-Test-Ban
Treaty (CTBT) 96

Index 113

Conca, Ken 107
Conference on Security and Cooperation in Europe (CSCE) 81, 87
Conflict Early Warning and Response Mechanism (CEWARN) 53–54
conflicts and violence 1–2, 3, 4; in Africa 50–56, 103, 104; and ASEAN 61–62, 71, 97; in Asia 65–68, 72–73; and the AU 42–43, 45, 46–48, 49, 56, 96; and civil society 101, 103; and climate change 2, 10–11, 13, 56, 105, 106; and the OAS 75–78, 92; and the OSCE 4, 5, 81, 83–86, 96; and SDG 16, 37–38, 39; and the UN 4, 9, 15–22, 30, 32, 36, 37–38, 39, 65, 96, 97, 104–105, 106
Contadora process 75
"contemporaneity" in human rights protection 26
Convention against Genocide 26
Convention against Torture 26, 63, 102
corruption 32, 35, 43–44, 64, 65, 77, 106
Costa Rica 76
Cote d'Ivoire 20–21
Council of Europe 87
cyber-security 68, 77

Dayton Agreement 85
de Alba, Luis Alfonso 11
democracy 22, 23, 24, 31, 32, 34, 35, 39, 91; in Africa 43, 46, 54, 56, 103–104; in the Americas 76, 77, 80–81; in Asia 62, 64, 65; in Europe 81, 86–89, 98; *see also* elections
Democratic Republic of the Congo (DRC) 48, 55
desertification 10, 29, 43, 55, 96
Dink v. *Turkey* 89
disarmament 1, 2, 3, 13–14, 29, 42–43, 95, 101; *see also* weapons of mass destruction (WMDs)
Disarmament, Demobilization and Reintegration (DDR) 45
discrimination 9, 31, 35, 79, 84, 87, 88, 90
diseases 77, 104–105
Doha 70
drugs 20, 68, 77, 78

East Asia 16, 45
East Asia Summit (EAS) 71
East China Sea 66
Economic and Environmental Committee 82
Economic Community of Central African States (ECCAS) 17
Economic Community of West African States (ECOWAS) 5, 6, 20, 37, 42, 52, 53, 56, 96, 97
education 24, 31, 64, 65, 69, 84, 96, 101, 102
Egypt 48, 97
El Salvador 97
The Elders 99–100, 103
elections 4, 17, 20, 48, 51, 87, 88, 97, 98; *see also* democracy
Endorois case 47, 49, 80, 89, 103
energy 11, 12, 13, 60, 67, 82; nuclear 10, 44, 47, 61; renewable 12, 13
Ennals, Martin 101
(in)equality 23, 29, 31, 54, 55, 64, 65, 90
Equatorial Guinea 17
Eritrea 97
Ethiopia 48, 51, 53, 54, 97
Europe 22, 66, 68–69, 82; democracy in 81, 86–89, 98; minorities in 4, 81, 83–86, 96, 98; *see also* Organization for Security and Cooperation in Europe (OSCE)
European Commission 90–91
European Committee for the Prevention of Torture 87
European Convention for the Prevention of Torture 26, 87
European Convention on Human Rights 87, 89
European Court of Human Rights (ECHR) 89–90
European Union (EU) 90, 101
explosive remnants of war (ERW) 46
extremism 17, 18, 19–20, 68, 69, 84; *see also* terrorism

Fall, Francois Lounceny 97
FemWise-Africa 47–48, 51
FIRST (Facts on International Relations and Security Trends) 101
food security 10, 11, 13, 18, 69, 86, 106
Forum for Security Cooperation 83

114 *Index*

France 105
Fund for Peace 4, 37, 39

Gabon 17
Gambia 20
gender issues 12, 17, 31; *see also*
women
General Assembly of the UN 3, 8, 9,
29, 32, 36, 37, 38, 61, 99–100,
105, 107
Geneva Center for Humanitarian
Demining (GICHD) 45–46
genocide 3–4, 24, 26, 46
Georgia 85
Germany 13
Getschel, Lindsay 13
Gísladóttir, Ingibjörg Sólrún 88
Global Campaign for Nature 12
Global Centre for the Responsibility to
Protect 99–100, 102
global warming 1, 2, 10, 11, 13, 29, 55,
96; *see also* climate change
Global Watch Over Human Security
29, 39, 91
governance 17, 20, 29, 31, 32, 43–44,
54, 62, 81, 87, 91, 98
Green Wall for the Sahara and Sahel
Initiative (GGWSSI) 43
greenhouse gases 10, 11, 80
Guinea 20, 52
Guinea-Bissau 52
Guinea, Gulf of 17
Guterres, Antonio (UN Secretary-
General) 2, 3–4, 8–9, 11, 13–14, 15,
18, 19, 20, 24–25, 36, 38, 68–69,
95–96

Haar, Barend ter 82
Hague Code of Conduct against
Ballistic Missile Proliferation
(HCOC) 83
"The Hague Recommendations
regarding the Education Rights of
National Minorities" 84–85
Hailu, Tigist 53
Haiti 75–76
Handyside Case (1976) 89
hate speech/crimes 22, 24–25, 87, 88
Helsinki Final Act (1975) 82, 86
High Commissioner on National

Minorities (HCNM) 3–4, 6, 81,
83–86, 91, 96, 98
High-Level Panel for the Sustainable
Ocean Economy 12
Honduras 97
Hong Kong 33
Hormuz, Strait of 65
Horn of Africa 97
human rights 1, 2, 5, 15, 37, 59, 69, 95,
98, 101, 102, 104, 107; in Africa 18,
20, 56–57, 98; and ASEAN 5, 59,
62, 63–64, 72, 97, 98; ASEAN
Intergovernmental Commission on
Human Rights (AICHR) 62, 63, 72,
97, 98; in Asia 19, 72, 91; and the
AU 4, 5–6, 42–43, 45, 46, 48–50, 57;
European Convention on Human
Rights 87, 89; European Court of
Human Rights (ECHR) 89–90; Inter-
American Commission on Human
Rights 76, 78, 80, 92, 98; Inter-
American Convention on Human
Rights 79; Inter-American Court on
Human Rights 78, 92; and the OAS
5, 6, 75–76, 78–81, 92, 98; Office for
Democratic Institutions and Human
Rights (ODIHR) 4, 6, 81, 86–87, 88,
91, 98; Office of High Commissioner
for Human Rights (OHCHR) 5, 26,
27, 28–34, 36, 39, 98, 107; and the
OSCE 3–4, 5, 81, 86–90, 91, 98; and
SDG 16, 8, 34–35, 37, 39, 64; treaty
bodies 25–26; and the UN 3, 4, 5, 8,
9, 16, 17, 22–34, 36, 38, 39, 69, 91;
UN Human Rights Council
(UNHRC) 16, 26–28, 31–32, 38, 98;
Universal Declaration of Human
Rights 23, 25, 31, 91
Human Rights Committee (UN) 25–26
Hyogo Framework for Action 43

India 5, 30, 66, 67, 68, 70, 71
Indonesia 60, 62, 63, 64–65
inequality *see* equality
"Institutional Building Blocks of Long-
Term Regional Security" 70–71
Inter-American Commission on Human
Rights 76, 78, 80, 92, 98
Inter-American Convention on Human
Rights 79

Index 115

Inter-American Court on Human Rights 78, 92
Inter-Congolese Dialogue 55
Intergovernmental Authority on Development (IGAD) 5, 6, 16, 37, 42, 53–54, 56, 96
Intergovernmental Panel on Climate Change (IPCC) 8–9, 10, 38
International Alert 99–100, 101
International Atomic Energy Agency (IAEA) 61
International Bill of Human Rights 25
International Commission on Intervention and State Sovereignty (ICISS) 3
International Court of Justice 107
International Covenant on Civil and Political Rights 25, 26
International Covenant on Economic, Social and Cultural Rights 25
International Crisis Group 6, 99–100, 101
International Institute of Strategic Studies (IISS) 100–101
international law 32, 61, 79, 102, 105, 108; of security and protection 6, 106–107, 108; and the UN 8, 9, 22, 23, 25, 29, 49–50
International Peace Institute (New York) 83
international security 29, 104, 105, 106–107, 108
Iran 59, 65, 70, 76
Iraq 19
ISIS/ISIL/Da'esh 19
Israel 65
Istanbul 86–87

Jakarta 62, 64, 71, 72
Japan 67, 70, 71
Joint Comprehensive Plan of Action (JCPOA) 65

Kamp, Christophe 81
Kazakhstan 17–18, 19, 68
Kenya 48, 53–54
Kissinger, Henry 106
Klass case (1978) 89
Krampe, Florian 43
Kyrgyzstan 17–18, 67, 68

Laos 63
Latin America 6, 22, 75, 76, 80
Latvia 89
Lavrov, Sergei 69
Liberia 20, 47, 52
Libya 48
Lord's Resistance Army (LRA) 17
Lusaka Peace Agreement 55

Machel, Graca 103
Madagascar 51
Malaysia 60, 63, 67
Mali 11, 18, 52–53
Mandela, Nelson 103
maternal mortality 27
McClintock, Elizabeth 81
McKibben, Bill 2
Middle East 4, 65, 66–67, 72–73
migration 11, 27, 29, 30, 37, 69, 105
Millennium Development Goals 30, 34
minorities 5–6, 30, 102; in Africa 5–6, 49, 57; in Asia 6, 62, 72; in Europe 4, 81, 83–86, 96, 98; High Commissioner on National Minorities (HCNM) 3–4, 6, 81, 83–86, 91, 96, 98
Minority Rights Group International 99–100, 102
Monitoring for Environment and Security in Africa (MESA) 43
Monroe doctrine 75, 78
Monrovia Declaration 52
Myanmar 60, 63

National Commission on Terrorist Attacks Upon the United States (9/11 Commission) 30
Network of Think Tanks and Academic Institutions 82
New Zealand 71
NGOs (nongovernmental organizations) 1, 26, 34, 36, 39, 54, 71, 98, 99–104; Fund for Peace 4, 37, 39
Niger 11, 18, 52–53
Nigeria 11, 17, 18, 20, 50
Non-Proliferation Treaty (NPT) 83
North Atlantic Treaty Organization (NATO) 10
North Korea 65, 66
nuclear energy 10, 44, 47, 61

116 Index

nuclear weapons 2, 5, 25, 44, 60, 61, 65, 66, 72, 80, 83, 96, 101; *see also* disarmament; weapons of mass destruction (WMDs)

Office for Democratic Institutions and Human Rights (ODIHR) 4, 6, 81, 86–87, 88, 91, 98
Office of Coordinator of Economic and Environmental Activities (OCEEA) 82
Office of High Commissioner for Human Rights (OHCHR) 5, 26, 27, 28–34, 36, 39, 98, 107
Organization for Security and Cooperation in Europe (OSCE) 3–4, 6, 37, 75, 81–91, 98; climate change 81–82; conflicts and violence 4, 5, 81, 83–86, 92, 96; human rights 3–4, 5, 81, 86–90, 91, 98; and SDG 16, 90–91; and WMDs 83
Organization of American States (OAS) 4, 5, 6, 75–81, 91, 97–98; and climate change 75–76, 80; conflicts and violence 75–78, 92; human rights 5, 6, 75–76, 78–81, 92, 98; and SDG 16, 81; and WMDs 77, 80
"Oslo Recommendations regarding the Linguistic Rights of National Minorities" 84–85

Pakistan 5, 66, 68
Panchsheel Treaty 61
Panel of the Wise (Panwise) 42, 47–48, 56, 96
Paris Principles 37
Peace and Development Advisors (PDAs) 21–22
Peace and Security Council (Arab League) 59
Peace and Security Council (AU) 5, 46, 47
peacebuilding 13, 15, 17, 38, 50, 51, 52, 75–76, 91, 101, 103–104, 106, 107; Department of Political and Peacebuilding Affairs (DPPA) 37, 96, 97; Peacebuilding Commission 38, 106; Peacebuilding Fund 20–21
peacekeeping 38, 47, 48, 52, 56, 75–76, 91, 103–104

peacemaking 5, 38, 48, 56, 62, 75–76, 91, 103–104
Pérez de Cuéllar, Javier 29
Persian Gulf 5, 59, 70
Philippines 60, 63, 65, 67, 101
piracy 17
pollution 11, 12, 81–82
poverty 29, 30, 42, 43–44, 62, 77, 104–105
prisoners 26, 37
Pritchard, Hamish 10

"quiet diplomacy" 33, 83–84

racial discrimination 31, 86
Rees, Martin 105
refugees 20, 30, 32–33; *see also* migration
renewable energy 12, 13
Republic of Congo 17
responsibility to protect 3, 31, 99–100, 102, 105–106, 107
Rio Treaty (Inter-American Treaty of Reciprocal Assistance 1947) 76, 77
Robinson, Mary 28, 103
Roma issues 87, 88
Romania 27
Rosenzweig, Cynthia 10
rule of law 4, 17, 23, 31, 32, 34, 35, 37, 46, 62, 64, 80–81, 84, 86–87, 89–90
Russia 10, 66, 67, 68, 69, 70, 71, 73, 76, 91
Rwanda 17, 24

Sachs, Jeffrey 42
Sahara 43, 52
Sahel 10–11, 16, 17, 18, 20, 43, 52
Sao Tome and Principe 17
Saudi Arabia 65, 70
sea levels 2, 10, 29, 30
Secretariat for Multidimensional Security (SMS) 77–78
Securing Our Common Future 2, 13–14, 15
Security Council of the UN 3, 6, 8, 12–13, 17, 21, 61, 65, 73, 83, 95, 98, 104–108; and the AU 51–52; and conflicts and violence 15, 16, 18, 19, 20, 37, 38, 65; and human rights 28, 30; and terrorism 30, 68–69

Index 117

Senegal 48
Serbia 85
Shanghai Cooperation Organization
(SCO) 59, 66, 68–69
Sharm El-Sheikh Commitments on
Water and Sanitation 43
Sierra Leone 52, 97, 101
Silencing the Guns 45, 51
Singapore 67
Sinti issues 87, 88
Sirleaf, Ellen Johnson 47
small arms and light weapons
(SALW) 45
Soering case (1989) 89
Somalia 53
South Africa 55, 103–104
South China Sea 65–66
South Korea 65, 70, 71
South Sudan 11
Southeast Asian Nuclear-Weapon-
Free-Zone (SEANWFZ) Treaty 61
Southern African Development
Community (SADC) 5, 6, 16, 37, 42,
51, 55, 56, 96, 103
Sri Lanka 101
Stockholm International Peace
Research Institute (SIPRI) 43,
99–100, 101
sub-regional offices of the UN 8, 16,
17–21, 38
Sudan 48, 51, 56
Survival International 99–100, 101
Sustainable Development Goal 16
(SDG 16) 2, 4, 8, 95, 98; and the
ASEAN 64–65, 72; and the AU
42–43, 50, 56; and civil society 4, 8,
34, 35–36, 37; conflicts and
violence 37–38, 39; human rights 8,
34–35, 37, 39, 64; and the OAS 81;
and the OSCE 90–91; and the UN 4,
34–38, 39
Sustainable Development Goals
(SDGs) 4, 30, 34, 36–37
Sweden 98
Syria 103

Tajikistan 17–18, 19, 68
Taliban 19
Tallin Guidelines on National
Minorities 85–86

terrorism 17, 18, 19–20, 24, 27, 29, 30,
35, 44–45, 47, 56, 68–69, 76–77, 78,
104–105
Thailand 60, 67
Thunberg, Greta 38, 39, 96, 98–100
Tlateloco, Treaty of 80
Togo 18, 52
torture 26, 63, 64, 78–79, 87,
99–100, 102
trade unions 37, 48
trafficking 17, 19–20, 45, 77; drug 20,
68; people 35, 37, 63, 64, 77, 102
transportation 12, 60, 67, 77, 82
tribal peoples 101
Trump, Donald 65, 91
Tunisia 48
Turkey 76, 86–87, 89
Turkmenistan 17–18, 19, 21
Tutu, Desmond 103

Uganda 53, 101
UN Assistance Mission in Afghanistan
(UNAMA) 19
UN Country Teams (UNCT) 21–22
UN Department of Political Affairs
(DPA) 21–22
UN Department of Political and
Peacebuilding Affairs (DPPA) 37,
96, 97
UN Development Programme (UNDP)
21–22, 96–97
UN Economic and Social Council
(ECOSOC) 24–25, 36, 38, 64
UN Economic Commission for Africa
(UNECA) 50
UN Framework Convention on Climate
Change Conference of the Parties
(UNFCC COP) 60
UN High Commissioner for Refugees
(UNHCR) 32–33
UN High Level Political Forum (HLPF)
36–38, 64
UN Office for Central Africa
(UNOCA) 17
UN Office for Disarmament Affairs
(UNODA) 14–15
UN Office for West Africa and the
Sahel (UNOWAS) 17, 18, 20
UN Panel on Climate Change
(UNPCC) 95–96

118 *Index*

UN Regional Centre for Preventive Diplomacy in Central Asia (UNRCCA) 17–18, 19–20, 21, 97
United Nations (UN) 1–3, 6, 8–41, 95–96, 101, 105–106; and the African Union (AU) 45–46, 47, 50, 51–52; and climate change 2–3, 8–9, 10–13, 38, 95–96; conflicts and violence 4, 9, 15–22, 30, 32, 36, 37–38, 39, 65, 96, 97, 104–105, 106; human rights 3, 4, 5, 8, 9, 16, 17, 22–34, 36, 38, 39, 69, 91; and international law 8, 9, 22, 23, 25, 29, 49–50; and SDG 16, 4, 34–38, 39; sub-regional offices of the UN 8, 16, 17–21, 38; and WMDs 3, 9, 13–15; *see also* Charter of the United Nations; General Assembly of the UN; Guterres, Antonio (UN Secretary-General); Security Council of the UN; sub-regional offices of the UN
United States 59, 65–66, 70–71, 72–73, 75, 76, 78, 89, 91, 97–98; *see also* Organization of American States (OAS)
Universal Declaration of Human Rights (1948) 23, 25, 31, 91
Universal Periodic Review 31–32, 63
Universal Rights Group 26
urbanization 43–44, 54
Uzbekistan 17–18, 19, 68

Velasquez Rodriguez Case (1988) 78–80
Venezuela 75, 92
Vieira de Mello, Sergio 31
Vietnam 60, 63
Vietnamese Boat People 33
Villagrán-Morales case (1999) 79

Viotti, Maria Luiza Ribeiro 51

water: management 21, 43, 82, 97; resources 10, 42, 53, 106
weapons of mass destruction (WMDs) 1, 2, 3, 4, 95, 96, 104–105; and ASEAN 60–61, 72; and the AU 42–43, 44–46; and the OAS 77, 80; and the OSCE 83; and the UN 3, 9, 13–15; *see also* biological weapons; chemical weapons; nuclear weapons
West Africa 5, 16, 17, 18–19, 20, 45, 96, 97; *see also* Economic Community of West African States (ECOWAS)
West Asia 16
women 20, 21, 24, 27, 47–48, 51, 56, 63, 64, 69, 88; *see also* gender issues
Working Group on Arbitrary Detention 27
Working Group on Enforced and Involuntary Disappearances 27
World Bank 45, 101
World Organization Against Torture (OMCT) 99–100, 102
Worldwatch Institute 99–100

Yemen 11
young people 1, 12, 13, 21, 51, 54, 69, 84–85, 88, 97, 98, 99–100; *see also* children

Zannier, Lamberto 85–86
Zarif, Mohammad Javad 70
Zdanoka v. *Latvia* 89
Zero Carbon Building for All 12
Zimbabwe 55, 56, 103
Zone of Peace, Freedom, and Neutrality (ZOPFAN) 60–61

Printed in the United States
By Bookmasters